RGO is deliberately taking an information-centric
~~Euro~~ American / Western view on Capitalism.
He acknowledges the Orient and its problem of capitalism
but the centre of Capital is still the West
I guess!

PRECARIOUS COMMUNISM

Manifest Mutations, Manifesto Detourned

GW00726130

Richar~~ Gilman-Opalsky~~

MINOR COMPOSITIONS

ISBN 978-1-57027-292-9

Cover design by New Collectivism / Irwin
Interior design by Margaret Killjoy

Released by Minor Compositions 2014
Wivenhoe / New York / Port Watson

Minor Compositions is a series of interventions &
provocations drawing from autonomous politics, avant-
garde aesthetics, and the revolutions of everyday life.

Minor Compositions is an imprint of Autonomedia
www.minorcompositions.info | minorcompositions@
gmail.com

Distributed by Autonomedia
PO Box 568 Williamsburgh Station
Brooklyn, NY 11211

www.autonomedia.org
info@autonomedia.org

Contents

I dedicate this book in loving memory to my father, Harry Opalsky (August 14, 1938 – July 15, 2011). From beginning to end, my father lived a precarious life. Yet, within every space of freedom, he embodied love, humor, and commitment, and lived without malice. I aspire to embody my father's love, humor, and commitment, in the ways that I can. I learned more from him than he ever knew.

INTRODUCTION:

Aims and Method of Communist Détournement [1]

THE AUTONOMIST MANIFESTO COULD NEVER BE WRITTEN. SUCH A thing is impossible, and would be rightly denied if it dared to announce itself. But one could write *an* autonomist manifesto, and under various titles, such manifestos have already been written. It is fair to say that this book, *Precarious Communism,* is a particular autonomist manifesto. To begin, the reasons for the book's subtitle – *Manifest Mutations, Manifesto Detourned* – must be explained.

This book is a détournement of Karl Marx and Frederick Engels' *The Communist Manifesto* of 1848 (written in late 1847, published in 1848). We therefore work primarily with what is manifest in another manifesto, including the logic of its arguments, as well as its particular and general aims. The present work also mutates the source material of the original manifesto, making a detourned manifesto, which is both a humble and audacious offering, a new manifesto that could be read entirely on its own.

In the absence of ideological fundamentalism, it is not possible to simply reject Marx. Critical communists, autonomists included, learn

---

1   I would like to thank Dylan Davis and Matt Bernico for their thoughtful and thorough review of an early version of the manuscript. I would also like to thank Heather Dell for her attention and conversation. Finally, Stevphen Shukaitis has been an invaluable and reliable friend of my work, and his feedback always makes it better.

from Marx and understand the importance and necessity of critical redeployments of his work. Hence, when Antonio Negri wrote *Marx Beyond Marx: Lessons on the Grundrisse* and *The Politics of Subversion: A Manifesto for the Twenty-First Century*, he understood the need to take Marx and Marxism out of the contexts of their various historical theorizations in order to make them speak to present times, beyond the limitations of their earlier days.[2] Indeed, many Marxists reject too much of the foundational Marxian lexicon, too many of the rudiments of Marx's system, to call themselves "Marxists" in any simple sense, and even the simplest senses of what it means to be a Marxist have been complicated by generations of slander, abuse, and the deceptions of various governments and ideologies. There is no simple sense of what it means to be a Marxist, and yet we cannot ignore Marx without revealing deficits in our own understanding. Marx's most serious opponents have long known that they cannot ignore him, and it is reassuring that he still has so many opponents today.

While I shall argue that the time for grand visions of an egalitarian future is over and done, I maintain that the revolutionary and utopian imagination does not belong to the archival domain of nostalgia. A utopian imagination has certain practical uses, even if some of its greatest old hopes are impossible. Revolution remains not only possible, but is in fact more practical than the plans of all those liberal dreamers who naively wish for a capitalist democracy free from the corruption of capital. So, the time for manifestos has not gone away. What we need is not a new unitary or final manifesto, but rather, a multiplicity of manifestos. Concretely, my question is: What is manifest in the manifesto today? But first, what is a manifesto?

The word "manifesto" derives from "manifest" and dates to 17th century Italian. For something to be manifest it must be presently perceptible and understandable. That which is manifest is discernible by our senses, registered as manifest within our conscious feelings and understanding, so a fundamentalist-materialist manifesto is a contradiction. For human comprehension, nothing is manifest without perception and understanding. Human comprehension only grasps that which was already manifest, *after* we have come to know it. Whatever is imperceptible, unknown, and misunderstood is not manifest, or at least, not yet manifest. The manifest content of a dream, as opposed to

---

2   Negri, Antonio, *Marx Beyond Marx* (Autonomedia/Pluto Press, 1991); *The Politics of Subversion* (Polity Press, 2005).

[handwritten: Awareness of problems of Communist Manifesto]

the elusive and vanished content the dream conceals, for example, distinguishes that which is manifest as that which is grasped or known. A manifesto seeks to explicate for others those things which its author feels to be manifest. Not all manifestos are equal – even the best ones have problems, even the best make mistakes. A manifesto manifests a series of articulations and arguments that seek to comprise an exclamatory work (a work that includes and supersedes analysis) – a manifesto does not wish to conceal its normative disposition. This book is a communist détournement, and no détournement is neutral.

Precarious Communism does provide analysis – cultural, social, political, and economical. But the present work also makes recommendations, and rethinks the purposes and demands of *The Communist Manifesto*. Those who we shall call "precarious communists" cannot unify a cohesive program for every radical desire expressed by (or embodied within) the multifarious humanity that condemns the existing state of affairs. That does not mean that we cannot outline agendas or make concrete demands. But demands are only ever developed as nodal points in the course of an evolving politics, and agendas can be revised in perpetuity to accommodate new articulations and intensifications of our desires (i.e., what we want). Politics doesn't end in the gratification of some one last desire.

[handwritten: Precarious communists use Marx's work to develop philosophy about today]

[handwritten: Precarious communists are non-vulgar who are skeptical about some of Marx's work e.g. there is]

* * *

It is also critical to provide from the outset a basic definition of "precarious communism," which will be further developed in the analyses of this book. *[handwritten: "proletariat"]* To begin thinking about precarious communism, we could start from any number of locations, but to take one, consider the communist epiphany of Anton Pannekoek in the early 1940s: "Now it is seen that socialism in the sense of State-directed planned economy means state-capitalism, and that socialism in the sense of workers' emancipation is only possible as a new orientation… New orientation needs time; maybe only a new generation will comprehend its full scope."[3] Fundamentally, the question of what is communism is a question of various – old, new, and possible – communist orientations, and today, it is a question of what to do with the communist disaffection of previous generations.

---

3   Pannekoek, Anton, *Workers' Councils* in *Left Communism Reader* (Prism Key Press, 2013), p. 433.

[handwritten: "New orientation" move away from state capitalism to letting workers control their work]

If we pay close attention to actually-existing revolt in the world, and do not force it into the frame of an ideological worldview (*Weltanschauung*), then we will not be able to conclude that new uprisings demand communist parties, socialist states, or some recast communist project from the 20th century. But general disinterest in communist forms from previous generations does not mean that there is no communist desire in the world today. What there is in fact is yet another stage in what Pannekoek called for over seventy years ago, "a new orientation," the emergence of new communist desires. Indeed, we could say that new communist orientations are inevitable, as there are numerous historical and theoretical examples to substantiate the claim.

Contrary to this, ongoing vilifications of communism continue to rely upon the same old pathological conflation of the whole Marxian corpus with statist catastrophe. This conflation has long been the fixation of so many conservatives, liberals, and anarchists alike. Yet through the haze of these pathological fixations, there is a nonetheless valid point about the horrific history of statist catastrophe. And although there have been many good grave-diggers working on the task, we must finally bury the ideologized anarchist-Marxist debate, *along with statism itself*, as casualties of the 20th century.

Still, there are many possibilities for what to do with communist desire in the face of communist disaffection. We could, for example, adopt some form of "anti-political" communism, or of the "nihilist communism" of Monsieur Dupont.[4] While Dupont's critique of radical optimism is necessary (and, I would say, the inevitable conclusion of honesty), and while communists can no longer be overly confident about some one alternative form of life or another, new communist orientations need not shift from optimism to nihilism, and need not surrender the whole political field to the failures and foreclosures of political parties and states. Meanwhile, there is no shortage of political content in the so-called anti-political tendencies, which is easily seen when we think the political against its conventional forms. It is more than fair to expect that we might have caught up by now with Foucault's old insistence on thinking the political in other ways and places than through sovereignty.

Largely, precarious communism describes the already-existing position of communists today, whose communism is neither

---

4   See Dupont, Monsieur, *Nihilist Communism: A Critique of Optimism in the Far Left* (Ardent Press, 2009).

- 5 -

well-characterized by confidence nor by nihilism. There is a vast terrain that separates the confidence of optimism from the oblivion of nihilism, but each side derives its assured conviction from a highly selective reading of positivity, on the one hand, or negativity, on the other. Precarious communism positions itself at various locations on the vast terrain in between optimism and nihilism. To argue *for* precarious communism is to argue for the importance of uncertainty in the theory and practice of radical milieus, and to defend the multiplicity, openness, and expression of communist desire against both capitalism and recurring tendencies on the Left to organize such desire into a unitary agenda that leaves our desires out.

To argue *for* precarious communism should not be confused with an acceptance of the whole fashionable discourse on precarity.[5] Most simply, precarious communism is a communism that lacks confidence about some particular, alternative future, but insists nonetheless on the unacceptable present and the unliveable future of the capitalist lifeworld. What it means to be a precarious communist is to be, as much as possible, a non-ideological communist who is honest about the past, present, and future. While ideology makes communism more confident, precarious communism is more philosophical, less ideological.

Precarious communism is *precarious* inasmuch as it accepts that concrete proposals for new ways of being-in-the-world will be differentially developed as nodal points within the contexts of actually-existing revolt. Precarious communism is *communist* on the grounds of its single most confident claim: A world organized by the logic of capital is a world organized against the diverse interests of most people on Earth.

5   Precarity refers to the condition or degree of our precariousness, that is, to the uncertain existence of persons, life, and the lifespans of social, political, and economic systems. The fundamental problem with the concept of precarity, or with the category of the precariat, is that they can be applied to everyone and everything, and therefore, may specify nothing in particular. For example, we can consider the precarity of even the least precarious people and institutions. What needs to be done, and what we shall be mindful to do throughout this book, is to distinguish different forms and causes of precarity, to understand and to insist that not all precarity is equally precarious. This is partly why, despite certain criticisms, we can never do away with class analysis or ideological analysis. Class analysis remains necessary to the analysis of different forms of precarity, just as ideological analysis is necessary to understanding why the precariat does not, and cannot, share a cohesive point of view.

As a more subordinate aim, this book is intended to help explore and develop détournement as a philosophical methodology, as a modality for a subversive writing within and upon already existing texts, and especially texts regarded by some to be canonical, classical, or even sacred. Here, I shall discuss the method of détournement as it is employed in this book, and then will not return to the question of methodology again. In the détournement of *The Communist Manifesto*, détournement will not be our subject matter. While this book is not primarily about methodology – which will be especially clear after the present Introduction – I emphasize the theory and purposes of its approach in recognition of the fact that détournement is a rather odd way to write a book, and even more, to think through philosophical questions.

Détournement always involves a kind of hijacking or rerouting of primary source material against itself, beyond its original intentions. For Guy Debord, détournement was theorized as part of a revolutionary project "undertaken within the present conditions of oppression, in order to destroy those conditions."[6] But what does that mean? Practically, détournement has mostly been explored as an activist methodology to be deployed on sonic, visual, filmic, commercial, or theatrical terrains, to make subversive use of readily available resources for the diverse purposes of radical criticism. Détournement has scarcely been explored as a philosophical methodology that makes subversive use of complete texts for the production of new ones; specifically, I mean the long-form détournement of classical or canonical works. There has been less sustained textual détournement, including the many fleeting detourned phrases peppered throughout Debord's *The Society of the Spectacle* or more substantially in Raoul Vaneigem's *A Declaration of the Rights of Human Beings*, the latter of which is comprised of creative rewritings of earlier declarations of rights, from the French Revolution and the United Nations. There are some other experiments in resonant veins, Michèle Bernstein's *All the King's Horses*, Stephen Duncombe's *Open Utopia*, A.C. Grayling's *The Good Book: A Humanist Bible*, and Alain Badiou's *Plato's Republic*, just to name some.[7] But all of these are fundamentally different from

---

6 Debord, Guy, "Perspectives for Conscious Changes in Everyday Life" in *Situationist International Anthology* (Bureau of Public Secrets, 2006), p. 98.

7 See Bernstein, Michèle, *All the King's Horses* (Semiotext(e), 2008); Duncombe, Stephen and More, Thomas, *Open Utopia* (Minor Compositions/Autonomedia,

the present project in ways too obvious to discuss. I have published two detourned texts.[8] Save for a few exceptions, the long-form détournement of philosophical text has been fragmentary, and mostly done for strategic and tactical reasons. This book was written on the premise that détournement has other uses beyond (not against) its more fragmentary applications.

Within the context of writing theory or philosophy, détournement functions on a level that hews closely to the methodologies of "immanent critique" and "deconstruction," but détournement is importantly different. I shall briefly provide some diacritical and positive clarifications.

The immanent critique of critical theory, at the heart of Theodor Adorno's "negativity," for example, accomplishes its critical aims by locating contradictions in the rules and logic necessary to the arguments that it wants to test, refute, or negate.[9] Immanent critique works by way of bringing out the contradictions of worldviews, philosophical traditions, or other systems of argumentation. In short, immanent critique brings objectionable logics to their breaking points.

In the hands of Jacques Derrida, deconstruction was a means to destabilize calcified narratives and conventional "readings" that had become authoritative to the point of intellectual authoritarianism. Derrida would read a text with seriousness and rigor against its conventional interpretation, which infuriated scores of philosophers who were employed as the guardians of "proper" interpretation. Derrida's deconstructions revealed that no text has a single meaning that stands apart from its reader. The reader of a text always and invariably does something to the text and to its meaning. Derrida insisted that "reading is transformational."[10]

For example, the US Constitution has been and can be read for or against conservative or liberal positions, as can be seen in Justice

---

2012); Grayling, A.C., *The Good Book: A Humanist Bible* (Walker Publishing Company, 2011); Badiou, Alain, *Plato's Republic* (Polity Press, 2012).

8   Chapter 4 of *Spectacular Capitalism: Guy Debord and the Practice of Radical Philosophy* (Minor Compositions/Autonomedia, 2011) is a détournement of Marx's *Theses on Feuerbach* and Part 3 of my "Unjamming the Insurrectionary Imagination: Rescuing Détournement from the Liberal Complacencies of Culture Jamming" (*Theory in Action*, Volume 6, No. 3, July 2013) also experiments with détournement as a method of sustained critique.

9   Most famously, see Adorno, Theodor *Negative Dialectics* (Continuum, 1983) and, with Horkheimer, Max, *Dialectic of Enlightenment* (Continuum, 1997).

10   Derrida, Jacques, *Positions* (University of Chicago Press, 1982), p. 63.

White's opinion on sodomy, in the Citizens United case, or in the dispute over the constitutionality of Barack Obama's health care reform act. Deconstruction seeks to take advantage of this openness, to expose the instability of, and ultimately to subvert, dominant ways of thinking about certain texts, including texts in philosophy, law, or even the sacred texts of religious traditions. For all of the criticisms that have accused Derrida of some kind of charlatanism, his work has always been two things: subversive and anti-authoritarian. Derrida is subversive in the sense that his work attacks and destabilizes what is easily or too easily accepted as the settled facts of knowledge, of texts and their meanings, and of those who claim to have expertise over them. His work is anti-authoritarian because it aims to show, precisely through its acts of subversion, that inasmuch as everyone reads or interprets the texts and symbols and images around them, everyone has a certain kind of power, and authoritative meanings are always subject to deconstruction.

So how does détournement extend beyond immanent critique and deconstruction? To begin with, détournement is not outside of or apart from the source it acts upon, and one can always see the traces of the original in the detourned work. A detourned work does not attempt to substantiate the grounds for an alternative reading, as in the case of deconstruction, for it prefers to make the source text say something that it most certainly does not say, but could or should say in light of different historical or political contexts or social problems.

In the 1956 "User's Guide to Détournement," Guy Debord and Gil J. Wolman state that there are "two main categories of detourned elements... These are *minor détournements* and *deceptive détournements*. Minor détournement is the détournement of an element which has no importance in itself and which thus draws all its meaning from the new context in which it has been placed. For example, a press clipping, a neutral phrase, a commonplace photograph. Deceptive détournement, also termed premonitory-proposition détournement, is in contrast the détournement of an intrinsically significant element, which derives a different scope from the new context."[11] In the first case, then, détournement is about utilizing other peoples' resources for entirely different purposes, taking what is available, regardless of its intended context, and making it say something else as you wish. In the

---

11   Debord, Guy and Wolman, Gil J., "A User's Guide to Détournement" in *Situationist International Anthology* (Bureau of Public Secrets, 2006), p. 16.

[handwritten margin notes: uses a normative argument and applies it a context showing that the argument should be twisted to say something different and relevant to the context]

second case, détournement addresses the intended context through some kind of critical derailment, making it turn on its self, contradict its claims, or extend in new directions. The present work utilizes both kinds of détournement, but mostly the latter given the significance of the primary source material.

I aim to develop détournement beyond the particular scopes of usage conceived for situationist praxis. On this point, it is necessary be blunt: This book is neither about détournement nor about Guy Debord and does not take special care to utilize détournement within the limits of any faithful commitment to Debord's own intentions, to the Situationist International (SI), or to the intellectual guardians of the SI today, the latter of whom are happy to function as museum guards (both figuratively and literally). The interest that I most share with Debord in this book, to which I am faithful for reasons other than his own, is an interest in projects "undertaken within the present conditions of oppression, in order to destroy those conditions."[12] Make no mistake; this book is about capitalism and its culture and crises today. This book is about communism and "communism," and about the prospects and limitations of the social production of power.[13]

Détournement always involves a rethinking, rerouting, and critical redeployment of primary source materials in order to make them speak to different historical and political contexts. What ultimately distinguishes détournement from immanent critique and deconstruction is: (1) Détournement does not want to bear out the total failure or refutation of the original it works with, for one selects a source for détournement precisely because of its acknowledged richness and possibilities, for the usefulness of its intrinsic material. This is particularly true in the case of the détournement of a complete text. Détournement

---

12   Debord, Guy, "Perspectives for Conscious Changes in Everyday Life" in *Situationist International Anthology* (Bureau of Public Secrets, 2006), p. 98.

13   I use "communism" in quotes to specify the vilified and deformed figure of communism that was prominent in the political discourses of the Cold War, that circulates again in the ideological narratives of today, and that is still widely utilized throughout the social and political sciences. "Communism," just to take one example, commonly conflates Marx with Stalin or socialism with the Soviet Union. I discuss the vilified and deformed figure of communism in relation to socialist philosophy and "spectacular socialism" in the Introduction and Chapter 3.1 of *Spectacular Capitalism* (Minor Compositions/Autonomedia, 2011). I also discuss "communism" more fully in Part II of the present work.

requires source materials worthy of détournement. Thus, détournement is not like the process of negativity and negation central to immanent critique. (2) Détournement does not want to demonstrate other possible readings of the source material, for it aspires to supersede its primary source material, revealing the limits of its applicability to other contexts than the ones in which and for which it was written. Détournement is interested in making texts speak against and beyond themselves, so that they say what must (or could and should) be said now. Thus, détournement is not the process of "transformational reading" central to deconstruction.

Positively, I have written a détournement of *The Communist Manifesto* because such an approach enables me (a) to rethink its strengths and weaknesses from a different historical, cultural, and political vantage point, and yet, from within its own *form* and *content*, leaving traces of the original in the new work; (b) to defend and to extend the best arguments of *The Communist Manifesto* through a creative rerouting of its logic and purposes, considering what it could and should say today; (c) to produce a peculiar companion text to the original, a text in which the original, or at least its ghost, still "appears," a text which identifies and replaces particular failures with different framings, analyses, arguments, and in some parts with different normative commitments.

* * *

When writing about *The Communist Manifesto* itself, I shall dispense with the tedious convention of attributing its authorship to both Marx and Engels. Indeed, Marx and Engels began working together on the *Manifesto*, and while Engels was in Paris, Marx worked on the *Manifesto* alone for roughly one month before Engels re-joined him. Beyond this real collaboration, it is important to note that Engels wrote his "Draft of a Communist Confession of Faith" in June of 1847, a text which contained many of the key terms and defining positions of the *Manifesto*. And before that, Engels had published his *The Condition of the Working Class in England* (1845). Nonetheless, Engels famously states in the Preface to the 1883 German Edition that the "basic thought running through the Manifesto... belongs solely and exclusively to Marx. I have already stated this many times; but precisely now it is necessary that it also stand in front of the Manifesto itself."[14] Given this, and the consistency of the *Manifesto* with the larger body of Marx's own work, I use the convention of referring to it as Marx's manifesto, and in light of Engels' qualification above, I shall consider myself duly justified in that decision.

The first English translation of the *Manifesto* was published in 1850. That was the first time that Marx's and Engels' names appeared on the publication. Earlier and numerous subsequent editions of the *Manifesto* were published under anonymous authorship. We would do well to remember that revolutionary manifestos ultimately depend upon the affirming attentions and energies of others who take up or express their positions in various ways, and that, therefore, manifestos always aspire to participate in movements outside of their pages, and so manifestos are neither really nor ideally the private property of their authors.

A brief note on sources: In this book, I am working with multiple editions of the *Manifesto*, often comparing them sentence by sentence. I am using the 1888 edition by Samuel Moore, the English translation that was made in cooperation with, and authorized by, Engels. The Moore translation has appeared in slightly different versions in the following editions, which are the ones I have used: The International Publishers pamphlet of 1948, 34th printing of the 100th anniversary edition, New York, 1994; The International Publishers Collected Works, Volume 6, Marx and Engels: 1845-48 edition, Progress Publishers, Moscow, 1976; The Pelican Book/Penguin edition, with the A.J.P. Taylor Introduction, published in 1967 in New York and the UK; The version published in Eugene Kamenka's *The Portable Marx* (Penguin, 1983); Finally, an on-line edition (marxists.org) proofed and corrected against the 1888 English translation by Andy Blunden in 2004. All of these versions are more or less the same, taking the Moore/Engels translation as their basis, but with different proofing, editorial corrections, and notes on alternative translations made by different editors and translators in the various editions. Some variations in the British and American English editions are also present. Full references for the editions I have directly quoted appear in the Bibliography, and unless otherwise noted, all page references in the endnotes refer to the International Publishers 1948 [1994] pamphlet edition.

---

14   Engels, Frederick, "Preface to the German Edition of 1883" signed London, 28 June, 1883, in *The Communist Manifesto* (Penguin/Pelican Edition, 1967), pp. 57-58.

Marx hated the use of his name for ideas he didn't propose!

Finally, it must be said that a 19th century Marx would denounce the very notion of this project. His words and their precise translation and treatment by others were of utmost importance to him. He did not live to see the 20th century, a century that betrayed his best ideas in every imaginable and egregious way. But we can know how offended Marx would be by the slightest rerouting of his arguments, because toward the end of his life, when more people were taking his ideas more seriously than ever before, he gave us his *Critique of the Gotha Programme* (written 8 years before he died).

The social democrats and liberals of The German Worker's Party stayed as close as they could to the meaning and tone of Marx's ideas, and Marx understood that intelligent people who read their program might not see the critical differences between his actual views and those of a political party that spoke a language of "Marxian" coloration. Another impetus, Marx and Engels were also falsely associated with having authored the Gotha Programme. But *Critique of the Gotha Programme* makes clear that Marx did not endorse, nor would he have accepted, anything "like" his arguments. Marx defended his own arguments against every close cousin in theory and praxis that, in his estimation, would threaten to disfigure or undermine his purposes and the purposes of the revolutionary movements of human history.

Today, there are still some residues of Marxist orthodoxy, for example, a stubborn insistence on making a Marxian class analysis even where insurgents are mobilized along other lines and where the proletariat is absent or invisible. But Marxist orthodoxy can always claim high ground in the justification provided by Marx himself in works like *Critique of the Gotha Programme*. Closer to my sensibilities, there has been another history of 20th century Marxism, including thinkers like Antonio Gramsci and Georg Lukács, on up to thinkers like Antonio Negri and Félix Guattari, who took creative liberties to rethink Marx beyond Marx's own rules and beyond the ideologizations of orthodox Marxisms.

From a certain point of view, this book is a little work of blasphemy, as I suppose the détournement of any great work would have to be. For the offended, I doubt that it will help to share my profound love and respect for the 1848 *Manifesto*. I doubt that it will help to emphasize that the 1848 *Manifesto* is a text especially worth detourning precisely because it is so complex, so beautifully written, philosophically rich, and still has so much to say about a world it could not have anticipated. To fundamentalists, the reality of reverence is no consolation for an act of blasphemy. And for the faithful descendants of all earlier orthodox Marxists, everything that follows may be upsetting.

Handwritten annotations:

We live in the society of the spectacle or spectacle capitalism in order to stop us thinking about actual reality, the system villifies its enemies in a spectacular ≠ (lie or not real) form Islam and, Communism in American history even what is British? What is not white?

First ≠ deceptive   Spectacle subject to its
Retournanent   society.
of
Marx's
Communist manifesto   " A spectre is haunting Europe
          "- the Spectre of communism."

Precarious Communism

WE ARE HAUNTED BY THE ACTUALLY EXISTING WORLD, WHICH WE can always (even if faintly) discern behind the spectacular and mythological luster of capitalism and almost a century of vilification of the communist idea. In the 1990s, no one would have said that the world was haunted by communism. There was a ghost but no haunting (not every ghost haunts). The world had been exorcised. It is perhaps surprising, then, that the specter of communism has been making a comeback, although the present form of what haunts us is not communism in any recognizable form, but its spectacle.

There is never only one specter doing the haunting. For a short while, the terrorist eclipsed the communist as the villain *par excellence*. Now, the terrorist haunts in the background, as the threat of communism reclaims center stage. In the 19th century, communism was a ghost indeed, in the 20th century it had a certain kind of materialization, a certain body, or many distinct, concrete embodiments. But its 20th century embodiments were killed, and communism returns "posthumously" as a kind of zombie. The real question of the return of communism today is if, perhaps finally, we might stop talking about the "return" of something that was once here, but rather, an emergence of the real thing, of some new thing, and not the old dead thing standing up again. The comeback we witness today is more what Marx called "the branding reproach of Communism," which functions anew as capital defends itself against any imaginable alternative in the midst of unprecedented crisis.[15]

Two things result from this situation:

> I. Communism remains in the world in two ways: First, as a scary idea, and second, as a *real* mode of expressing generalized disaffection. When people occupy city parks and buildings, they are called "communists" by their enemies, and the name fits well in both ways.
>
> II. It is time for communists to openly, in the face of the whole world, assert a precarious communism, to become more and more autonomist, with many manifestos, and too ungovernable for any grand unification.

[handwritten margin notes: "they aren't Marxists just ppl protesting about life"; "its got to be individual not one bible"]

To this end, we could begin with Gilles Dauvé's premise: "Communism is not a programme one puts into practice or makes others put into practice, but a social movement... Communism is not an ideal to be realized: it already exists, not as a society, but as an effort, a task to prepare for... The discussion of communism is not academic. It is not a debate about what will be done tomorrow. It is an integral part of a whole series of immediate *and* distant tasks, among which discussion is only one aspect, an attempt to achieve theoretical understanding."[16]

[handwritten notes: "abolition of private property" (Marx); "abolishing the present state of things" (Marx); "disarmament"; "using RGO Da's; its not those quotes but those campaigning"; "for a socialist society"; "social movements"]

---

15   Marx, Karl, *The Communist Manifesto* (International Publishers, 1994), p. 8.

16   Dauvé, Gilles and Martin, François, *The Eclipse and Re-Emergence of the Communist Movement: Revised Edition* (Antagonism Press, 1974), p. 17.

[handwritten: Surely there is a consistent struggle between real and the the spectacular at least sub-conciously?]

More or Less Anxious

[handwritten: historical materialist? statement too vague afterwards to discen]

(Struggle and Its Discontents)

[handwritten: agree with Marx]

MARX WAS RIGHT ABOUT HISTORY, BUT STRUGGLE IS OVERRATED.

Marx was right that "oppressor and oppressed" have "stood in constant opposition to one another" throughout human history, that they have "carried on an uninterrupted, now hidden, now open fight, a fight that each time ended, either in a revolutionary reconstitution of society at large, or in the common ruin of the contending classes."[17] Struggle happens. Struggle is inevitable. But struggle is not what anyone desires to do. *[handwritten: critique of Marx]*

The wealthiest people "struggle" against neuroses, compulsions, pathologies and other psycho-social maladies attached to their positions. The most secure among us struggle against an anxiety about the prospects of losing their position, and they struggle against a fear of the insubordination of those they depend upon. All struggles are not equal, but all of us struggle against various forms of precarity, anxiety, mass depression, alienation, misery, and from material want and insecurity. Julia Kristeva explains the generalized psycho-social condition well: "Faltering images of identity (when they're not lacking altogether) and lost confidence in a common cause, gives rise at the national level to

---

17   Marx, op. cit., p. 9.

[handwritten: people don't always have desire to struggle] [handwritten: does this attack logic of precarious communists?]

of how this relates to struggle and its critique and whether @ RGO has misinterpreted Marx?

just what the depressed individual feels in his isolation: namely, feeling cut off from the other person (your nearest and dearest, neighbors, politics) and from communication, inertia, your desire switched off. On the other hand, people who rebel are malcontents with frustrated, but vigorous desires."[18] In between moments of rebellion, there is also a struggle against the clinical condition of everyday life. Kristeva later says: "I have found that many of my patients suffer from new configurations of pathologies that I call 'the new maladies of the soul.'"[19]

Struggle is indeed the content of history, but it is not the sole content. The other side of struggle is desire, aspiration, longing. One might say that this other side is only part of struggle, that it is only what motivates struggle, the engine of struggle. That is not true. Desire exists also in the absence of struggle; it guides and animates us whenever no external imposition is present. Desire can motivate struggle, yes, but neither is a prerequisite for the other. People can and do often struggle in the opposite direction of their desires, and desire can function well (as a motivation for conscious human action) without struggle. Desire can be autonomous from struggle, and that is perhaps our greatest desire.

Raoul Vaneigem has done better than anyone else to diagnose the relationship between pleasure and desire on the one hand, and capitalism on the other. Gilles Deleuze and Félix Guattari are typically credited more for developing this diagnosis, and not undeservedly, but they have wanted to own that characterization far less than Vaneigem has. Deleuze especially, has reacted against being seen as a philosopher of desire.[20] Vaneigem, on the other hand, wrote *The Book of Pleasures*, never considered it a misconception to be regarded an open advocate of insurrectionary desire, and must not be overlooked for his diagnosis of our disfigured libidinal energy.[21]

Vaneigem held that the "materiality of capitalism... reduced the entity God to the 'nature' of things; and it was in man's 'nature' to make it productive, and profitable."[22] Vaneigem precisely uses the term "*market perspective*, to describe the state in which pleasure is repressed

---

18   Kristeva, Julia, *Revolt, She Said* (Semiotext(e), 2002), pp. 83 and 84.
19   Ibid., p. 128.
20   See Deleuze, Gilles, "D as in Desire" in *Gilles Deleuze From A to Z* (Semiotext(e), 2012).
21   Vaneigem, Raoul, *The Book of Pleasures* (Pending Press, 1983).
22   Vaneigem, Raoul, *The Movement of the Free Spirit* (Zone Books, 1998), p. 23.

Pleasure

Does amusement count as pleasure?

Pleasure vs work - separated

because it is seen as a force hostile to work and to the civilization of work. It is a state in which life degenerates into survival; and pleasures, carefully proscribed, appear only as mortal wounds."[23] And: "Desire is under an eternal, unremitting curse to punish itself for not being profitable – a curse never to be lifted so long as individuals remain in this state of alienation that makes them strangers to themselves, and so long as they construct the image of a God of terror and of consolation, a God of retribution who must be paid and who pays in return."[24]

2 sides to God

What this means is that human desire was a casualty of capitalism, even before one could speak of revolutionary struggle. Desire is a longing that embodies real human aspirations, whereas pleasure is an affective state, a feeling from gratified desire. Vaneigem considers that the market perspective and profit-logic of capital are hostile to desire and pleasure, the latter of which are variously repressed, proscribed, and punished as potentially dangerous social forces. Accordingly, he argues in defense of the restoration of desire and the pursuit of pleasure, in direct contrast to the historic valorization of struggle that has been so central to revolutionary theory, including to that of many forms of Marxism. Capitalism does not only separate the haves from the have-nots, setting them up for some grand antagonism on the horizon, for it also separates people from their desires. Expropriation, in other words, has an affective and psychological side. And, Aristotle and John Stuart Mill were on the right track when they identified immediate or future pleasures as the ends for which we act.[25]

It's not our desire or pleasure but it's the one of our capitalist selves

Present-day post-industrial, post-Fordist, finance-capital societies have not done away with the class antagonisms Marx diagnosed. Hence, we still need to do class analysis and consider the ever-changing state of class consciousness. But our post-industrial, post-Fordist realities have fragmented, bifurcated, and internally diversified class identifications, so that class is now but one cleavage amongst others, more or less relevant in light of particular contexts. Class analysis guarantees nothing, not even a good understanding of what is happening in the real world of human conflict, and class identity is not the only (or even necessary) potentially revolutionary self-understanding. A person's level of anxiety,

Not just class but look at class →

---

23 Ibid., p. 27.
24 Ibid., p. 28.
25 For the place of pleasure in Aristotle, see Weinman, Michael, *Pleasure in Aristotle's Ethics* (Continuum, 2007); For Mill, see Mill, John Stuart and Bentham, Jeremy, *Utilitarianism and Other Essays* (Penguin Books, 1987).

Détournement of Marx?

human is only human when he is at home engaging in animal functions?

[handwritten: we don't know what we exactly and really desire]

alienation, or precariousness does not correspond directly to their level of material security in everyday life. In a crucial twist, those two things (1. anxiety/alienation/precariousness and 2. materiality) have shown their capacity to liberate themselves from each other.

[handwritten: Détournement of Marx critique of Marx]

Our epoch, the epoch of generalized anxiety, possesses, however, this distinctive feature: While we have less hope in any particular idealized future, we have greater disaffection for the present state of affairs. We do not know what we want, often as individual persons as well as in any given collective modality, but there are widespread indications that the existing state of affairs is immoral, or, if you prefer, unsustainable and unstable, and thus increasingly unacceptable.

[handwritten: Détournement of Hegel]

With a daily repression of desire and the punishment of pleasure in everyday life (i.e., work), we have come to accept the unacceptable, to tolerate the intolerable, to rationalize the irrational, and to sustain the unsustainable. At the same time, it is rather easy to disclose that most everyone confesses the irrationality of certain arrangements in the relations of power, of the agenda for a "reasonable" life of work and reward. The problem has been that, once we make the confession, we recoil at the impracticality and danger of rejecting the intolerable. Nonetheless, there have been recent signs in Greece, the UK, Syria, Egypt, Tunisia, Spain, Brazil, Turkey, and Thailand, and even in the US, amongst other places, that human beings may not continue to accept the unacceptable in perpetuity.

[handwritten: détour nement of Marx no material spring]

From where do the latest insurrectionary impulses spring? They do not really "spring" up from anywhere. We must consider that the current era of anxiety was in an incubation phase for almost two decades, from the end of the Cold War until roughly 2008, when the economic crisis opened up on the global public sphere. Consider what has been called the short 20th century, from 1914 to 1989, by Jürgen Habermas and others.[26] The short 20th century was marked by catastrophic events, by world war, by revolution and the formation of the Soviet Union, followed by decades of "communist" projects, masses of bodies herded together for movement or massacre, and the transformative events of 1989 to 1991. Framed along these lines, the 20th century has largely been construed as a century defined by a grand stand-off between "communism" and capitalism.

---

26 See "Learning from Catastrophe? A Look Back at the Short Twentieth Century" in Habermas, Jürgen, *The Postnational Constellation: Political Essays* (The MIT Press, 2001), p. 43.

Spectacular

In the first decade thereafter, in the 1990s, "communism" had been variously disappeared, exhausted, and abandoned, or simply inarticulate, speechless, and defenseless. But increasingly into the "postsocialist" era, we could not resist a certain question: After GATT, NAFTA, CAFTA, FTAA, WTO, and other institutional developments (i.e., the Maastricht Treaty), we had to ask: Was capitalism the only operational logic alive in the world? Surely, the organizational modes of capitalism were changing, but its operational logic had overcome the material and ideological impediments of the 20th century, and now appeared without a rival. At the same time, all the old problems were present and growing. *Unsure as to whether state capitalism + free market capital is diff logic*

A breaking point was perhaps not inevitable, but came enthusiastically out of the mountains of Chiapas, Mexico, with the Zapatista uprising of 1994. After this, the reintroduction and resonance of Marxist ideas and various other critiques of capitalism were on a slow rise, gradually more widespread, and once again, increasingly being taken seriously. To take one example, at a certain point in recent years, the self-proclaimed communist philosopher and Lacanian psychoanalyst, Slavoj Žižek, became a bona fide celebrity who could pack auditoriums as (or more) quickly and reliably as international pop stars. Even his recent tome about Hegel (*Less Than Nothing: Hegel and the Shadow of Dialectical Materialism*) has not dissuaded widespread interest in his lectures, which prominently feature critical denunciations of capitalism. In this context, Žižek is an important sign, an indication of a possibility. Substantive assessments of his work aside (and they do not appear in this book), the possibility for an openly communist public intellectual to be taken as seriously as Žižek provides at least some evidence that the capitalist mythology is not a totality.[27] Throughout this work, we shall consider other and better examples of diffuse and palpable communist desire.

determinant based on possibility and signs not as material but idealism spread of ideas and recognition of those real not spectacular ideas.

(New Expropriations of Brains from Bodies)

The bourgeoisie, or whatever we will call the class of persons that commands the lion's share of wealth and power safeguarded by the law,

---

27 We could consider other openly communist public intellectuals or figures, but at the time of this writing, Žižek stands out as a uniquely high-profile example.

still exists, and is today comprised of even fewer numbers. But class is more elusive now, and the forces of labor and law have seen their physicality eclipsed by a psychic dimension. Marx understood colonization by way of material and physical force, yet neo-colonialism now operates largely in a biopolitical way, in addition to by means of foreign policy. Propaganda and policy are increasingly surpassed by psycho-social developments with physical stakes.

Let us consider a clear case of an elusive psycho-social development with clear stakes: Remember the eight-hour workday – that transformative achievement fought for by anarchists and communists and the labor movement. It was a hard-won achievement, triumphant wherever it occurred, against the will of capitalist bosses. But the eight-hour workday is over. The eight-hour workday has been ended, without a fight, and with the inadvertent complicity of working people. The eight-hour workday has been replaced by the maximal-length workday, the workday of the wakeful state. The conscious energy of workers is now available for extraction at all wakeful times, interrupted sleep becomes work time, and actual sleep coincides with the time needed to recharge cellular devices.

But what, exactly, has happened? This major transformation in everyday life was, at least from the point of view of everyday people, a kind of accident, an unplanned surrender of our conscious energy to work and its psychological comportment. And work has been increasingly cognitized. This development in the working lives of everyday people was superbly studied by Manuel Castells in his excellent trilogy *The Information Age: Economy, Society, and Culture.* In the third volume, *End of Millennium,* Castells writes:

> The information technology revolution induced the emergence of informationalism, as the material foundation of a new society. Under informationalism, the generation of wealth, the exercise of power, and the creation of cultural codes came to depend on the technological capacity of societies and individuals, with information technology as the core of this capacity. Information technology became the indispensable tool for the effective implementation of processes of socio-economic restructuring. Particularly important was its role in allowing the development of networking as a dynamic, self-expanding

form of organization of human activity. This prevailing, networking logic transforms all domains of social and economic life.[28]

Castells also observes how physical labor is increasingly conducted by cognitive means, as the automation of repetitive tasks is increasingly carried out remotely by way of computer management. This is also one of the defining features of what Alain Touraine called the "post-industrial society."[29] The old physicality of certain forms of work remains, particularly in mass production factories, construction, sanitation work, and throughout the service sector. It is true that capitalist societies have worked to hide the gruelling physicality of work, by creating as many "invisible" sites for them as possible, often achieved by concealing workers in private plants or by moving whole operations to remote outsourced locations. The old physicality of work remains, and yet, it is viewed as a problem to be solved. Following Foucault, we could say that the everyday life of work is more and more a system in which brains control bodies.[30]

But this is not the more elusive side of the psycho-social development we've been discussing. The real trick of the maximal-length workday was that it packaged the complete takeover of our wakeful state as a gift of time. Similar to how capitalist writers sang the praises of the departure from feudalism as the worker's liberation to free labor, informationalism was ushered in with other freedom stories. But the conversion of time to the cellular format has had many casualties. The cellular format of time is a development that Castells could not have foreseen very well during his study of the information age in the late 1990s. The cellular development in time involves total access to the conscious energies of everyday people, and aims for a total "liberation" of conscious energy from geographic and bodily impediments. In other words, this new regime moves beyond the system of brains controlling bodies, toward a system of disembodied brain activity, which relegates the body to a kind of sensory-sexual apparatus that only requires maintenance.

28 Castells, Manuel, *The Information Age: Economy, Society, and Culture, Volume III, End of Millennium: Second Edition* (Blackwell Publishers, 2000), pp. 367-368.

29 Touraine, Alain, *The Post-Industrial Society: Tomorrow's Social History: Classes, Conflicts and Culture in the Programmed Society* (Random House, 1971).

30 See Foucault, Michel, *Power/Knowledge: Selected Interviews and Other Writings 1972-1977* (Pantheon Books, 1980) and *The Birth of Biopolitics: Lectures at the Collège de France, 1978-1979* (Palgrave Macmillan, 2008).

While natural and cognitive scientists, and neuropsychologists, including people like Sam Harris and Richard Dawkins, as well as the philosopher Daniel Dennett, have been reinforcing the nonexistence of any mind-body split, while they have been busy explaining everything in the world on the premise that mind is matter, that the human brain is entirely bodily, capitalism has been working out a new horizon that they have completely ignored. In all of the blasphemous discourses of these thinkers, capitalism has been treated as a nonissue, as something to accept without question, for it simply is. Meanwhile, capitalist informationalism has managed to extract brain activity from the rest of the body, so that, even in a consistently materialistic way, ideation and thought could be distilled and extracted as an immaterial content.

This does not refute the empirical claims of cognitive science. Brain function is indeed bodily, but from the perspective of capital, that fact is considered a problem. The apparatus of the body, which supports the brain, is far too limiting. Why must the whole body be carried around just to bring its brain activity to some one place or another? The tedious human body must be carried around from place to place, fed, and paid for in its movement on planes and trains and inside of costly cars, all of which are too slow. The body needs a place to sleep, requires physical space, and gets tired even before the brain is done thinking. Five-hour energy drinks are not the best solution to this problem. Capital fully grasps, and is attempting to overcome, the problem so sharply observed by Eric Hobsbawm: "Human beings are not efficiently designed for a capitalist system of production."[31] As part of the effort to solve this problem, capitalism effectuates a peculiar kind of mind-body split, as cellular developments have managed to get brain function to go mobile, to travel freely and fast, in real time, without the physical mass of the body itself. While the cognitive and neurosciences have very well established the mind as the body, capitalism has achieved a functional separation of the two. And none of this interests neuroscience. This is why, even when science infuriates theology, it doesn't bother capitalism in the slightest. When Dennett wrote his well-known book with the most audacious title, *Consciousness Explained*, he set out to give us consciousness in purely materialist

---

31   Hobsbawm, Eric, *The Age of Extremes: 1914-1991* (Abacus Publishing, 2004), p. 414.

terms, and to consider the philosophical implications of this.[32] It is both interesting and disturbing that the explanation of consciousness does not, from his point of view, require any consideration of human consciousness in the context of the political-economic dimensions of everyday life.

Practically, what cellular time does is obliterate time "after work." In your pocket, always on your person, messages find you. En route to the grocery store, playing with your sons and daughters, the demands of capital and work can intervene. Of course, there are other and far more benign applications, social, familial, cultural, public, and political. But these applications have been overemphasized and overdetermined by overzealous optimists. What has got to be grasped more centrally is the structural transformation of everyday life in the interests of capital. What has got to be grasped more centrally is that the obligations and anxieties of work can reach you everywhere, at any moment during your wakeful state. You make a stand. You do not reply until Monday morning, but your psyche is already colonized, you anticipate the work, which has announced itself as an obligation in advance, and it colors your relaxation, such that everything that is not the work you've postponed becomes nothing more than a diversion.

[handwritten margin note: Blurring lines between work and rest]

How flippant and pompous are those rebuttals that say that you could avoid all this because you don't have to succumb to cellular time? Yes, you don't have to drive a car, use a telephone, and own a computer, but that is true only in the most reductionist sense of choice. You can live the way the Amish used to, but nowadays, if a young person does this as an experiment – ninety days of being "unplugged" – it becomes a news story, because it is so exceptionally rare.[33] After the experiment, there is a sensible expectation to return to a functional social life, plugged in to the associational surrogates that define human interaction today. At a certain point, such experiments become banal, and one cannot even be said to be proving a point by abstaining from computers.

We must understand that informationalism in cellular time is not a simple "use" in the sense of the deployment of tools. It is not even about technology in the end. It is about intersubjectivity,

32   Dennett, Daniel C., *Consciousness Explained* (Back Bay Books, 1991).

33   See "Jake Reilly's 'Amish Project:' 90 Days Without a Cell Phone, Email and Social Media" cited at http://news.yahoo.com/90-days-without-cell-phone-email-social-media-015300257.html (Accessed, 12/28/2012).

communication, inclusion, understanding, information, and indeed, about being-in-the-world. We should speak about the ontology of cellular time, because we are not talking about technology, but being. We are either a participant in the networked society or not, and at a certain stage of its development, we can no longer choose, for such choosing becomes a deprivation of human relationality that confounds our sociality as human beings living in the world. What Immanuel Kant said about the inevitable ascendancy of cosmopolitanism seems more immediately applicable to the assimilation of life to informationalism and cellular time, in that it relies upon "the very nature of things to force men to do what they do not willingly choose (*fata volentem ducunt, nolentem trahunt*)."[34]

The old systems of relationality, in which topical common space was idealized, in which the agonistic ideal was to come together in actually embodied communities, no longer holds in the epoch of brains liberated from bodies. Cellular time has abolished the eighthour workday. To the extent that free time can be found anywhere on Earth, it is now being colonized just as geographic space once was, and time is disappearing. The iconic memory of the Haymarket Affair, and what it meant to everyday people around the world, will become a new kind of curiosity, because the workers themselves have unwittingly opted (in the Kantian sense above) for the maximal-length workday of the wakeful state. This was not stupidity. We thought we were being given the gift of time, but ended up giving it all away.

Marx developed the first, and still one of the best, critical theories of globalization. He wrote in 1848 that "Modern industry has established the world market" and about its "immense development to commerce, to navigation, to communication" which "in its turn, reacted on the extension of industry; and in proportion as industry, commerce, navigation, railways extended, in the same proportion the bourgeoisie developed, increased its capital, and pushed into the background every class handed down from the Middle Ages."[35] Marx's understanding of the necessarily globalizing tendencies of capital cannot be gainsaid. Developments over the past 160 years have shown capitalism to be irrevocably growth-oriented, an inevitable orientation that stems from the logic of accumulation. And Marx understood well that the greatest revolutions had been made by his enemies. But the

---

34   Kant, Immanuel, *Political Writings* (Cambridge University Press, 1999), p. 92.
35   Marx, op. cit., p. 10.

problems of capitalism ultimately rest on its logic of accumulation and the necessity for perpetual growth.

In the context of informationalism and cellular time, one could see how it would be difficult to speak of the "intrinsic neutrality" of technology. After all, we have been speaking of *capitalist* technology developed and adopted in the interests of accumulation and perpetual growth. Nonetheless, John Zerzan is wrong to vilify technology just as Murray Bookchin was wrong to accept its liberatory dimensions.[36] The issue is not technology, but its operational logic. Technology is not intrinsically neutral because it exists in its many current forms as the result of research, design, development, and implementation governed by the logic of capital. Automation has not been developed in a communist way, which is to say, in order to shorten the workday to three hours long, let alone to abolish an everyday life of work. Well after mass production technologies had begun proliferating throughout the Industrial Revolution, the workday stayed as long as it was, and was even extended, because the technology was developed and implemented to maximize the extraction of workers' energies. It is too simplistic to say that this is merely the capitalist use of intrinsically neutral technologies that could be used in a communist way, because the technologies we now have were researched, designed, and developed for particular uses, and they cannot easily or reliably be used against their specific intentions. The purpose and design of technologies delimit their range of possible applications, and they can only be repurposed within those limitations.

Can we imagine alternative or communist deployments of capitalist technologies? Yes, and there are numerous examples of activists and radicals who have made subversive use of capitalist technologies. But there are at least three things to keep in mind here: (1) First, subversive uses of technology are not autonomous inasmuch as they are dependent upon the provision of services by capitalists. Such services are provided, regardless of our use, only to the extent that our "subversive" uses do not contradict the interests of capital. Often, these services can be firewalled, cancelled, or "switched off" at the discretion of capital, more than they already are, as circumstances demand. (2) Second, we make subversive use of technologies that we did not research, design,

---

36　See Bookchin, Murray, "Towards a Liberatory Technology" in *Post-Scarcity Anarchism* (Black Rose Books, 1986), and Zerzan, John, "Against Technology" in *Running on Emptiness: The Pathology of Civilization* (Feral House, 2002).

or develop. Thus, our "individuated" uses are nonetheless always already standardized. An interesting case is that of the replacement of MySpace with Facebook. A voluntary exodus from MySpace to Facebook decimated the former "social networking" platform, making the latter an almost-universal metatopical common space. MySpace allowed for more personalization, Facebook allowed for less. MySpace provided more opportunities for users to engage in what one might call "a democratic manipulation" of their page and its content. Yet, the clean and standardized space of Facebook won out in the end. (3) Third, any good subversive use of technology must be measured against an honest accounting of the transformation of our sociality, as, for example, we have discussed above in relation to informationalism and cellular time.

On the other hand, we cannot accept the vilification of technology as written, for example, in the works of Zerzan. The vilification of technology writ large romanticizes earlier forms of sociality, as Zerzan's primitivism has always done as a matter of definition. Zerzan works out of anthropological research on "primitive" human associations, and is thus very clear about the dangerous instrumentality of all technological development. His view is self-consciously and proudly totalizing, as this is the central means by which he distinguishes his perspective as being the "most radical." Zerzan's perspective even romanticizes a personal aversion to technology. Yet such an aversion is increasingly untenable, even for primitivists, and this is not a matter of hypocrisy or commitment on their parts, but rather, of possibility.

Technology is not totalitarian, because power has no need for totalitarianism anymore. Existing power relations function and survive far better with flexibility and by way of making tolerable allowances for autonomous action. It is true that technology in all of its current guises is squarely on the side of capital, determined at every stage of its research, design, development, and deployment, but this only controls what must be controlled. Technology has, both intentionally and inadvertently, left countless open spaces. Chelsea Manning, Julian Assange, and WikiLeaks have shown us this. Much earlier, in 1994, the Zapatistas seized upon technological open space in indispensable ways and to great effect. We need not suggest anything absurd, i.e., that technological open space will undermine capitalist technology by mistake, or that such should be the aspiration of subversives. Instead, I want to insist that we retain a focus on the ontological questions of technology, as analysed above, on the changing state of being-in-the-world – what could be called "technontology" – and not on technology per se.

how technology) affects what we do (being)

(The Ubiquitous and Insecure Logic of Capital)

Each step in the development of capitalist technology was accompanied by a corresponding development of the shrinking and growing bourgeoisie. "Shrinking and growing" is the only way to properly speak of the bourgeoisie, or whatever name one gives to the least precarious among us. That class is shrinking in numbers, but growing in terms of its consolidated influence.

The influence of capitalist businessmen is always political, as Marx argued in 1848, and C. Wright Mills proved beyond any shadow of a doubt in his 1956 book, *The Power Elite*.[37] Yet, throughout the world, especially in the UK and the US, there is still incessant talk about market versus state forces, as if the two were independent foes. The 2012 US presidential election hinged almost entirely on this single lie. But Marx understood well that "the bourgeoisie has at last, since the establishment of modern industry and of the world market, conquered for itself, in the modern representative state, exclusive political sway. The executive of the modern state is but a committee for managing the common affairs of the whole bourgeoisie."[38] The fake libertarians of the US never tire of their foolish claim that the liberal government wants to manage the economy, when in fact the liberal government has given itself entirely over to the economy, has made itself beholden by law to the wishes of capital, and continues to be steered by a consortium of capitalists. Fake libertarians rabidly spout off against intrusive governments, while governments worldwide have opened themselves up to intrusion, in some cases begging for it. As Marx and Mills understood well, over a century apart, government has happily served the private sector and helped hammer the final nails into the coffin of public administration. In the US, liberals worked hard to dismantle the Aid to Families with Dependent Children program, inaugurated NAFTA, integrated fully into the WTO, and rescued capitalist banks

37   Mills, C. Wright, *The Power Elite* (Oxford University Press, 1956).
38   Marx, op. cit., p. 11.

and auto companies who benefitted just as much from corporate welfare under the rule of liberals as they did under that of conservatives. For all of this, for being the very best friend that capitalism has ever had, such governments are accused of Marxism.

Even in an epoch of capitalist crisis, capitalism has got the upper hand. Even in states of financial collapse, it is still capitalism that is called for a way out. If BP destroys large segments of the Gulf Coast ecosystem, we demand that BP saves it. On the one hand, we say that they are responsible for repairing the damage that they caused, but on the other hand, we cannot think of anyone else capable of managing the disaster.

Capitalism has far surpassed the old replacement of personal worth and use-value with exchange-value, which Marx wrote about in the *Manifesto*. We have seen the emergence of what Jean Baudrillard called "the political economy of the sign" and the emergence of a whole cultural regime of sign-values.[39] Beyond redefining the meaning of freedom to "free trade," we have also come to speak of freedom in terms of consumption within the context of the social signification embedded in the sign-values of various patterns of consumption. Baudrillard is useful for many reasons, not the least of which being his contribution to understanding a history of increasingly intimate relationships with objects. Marx worried about "naked, shameless, direct, brutal exploitation," but today, this is obscured once again, as the nature of our exploitation is more subtle, psycho-social, integrated into our everyday relationality.[40] Exploitation, wherever it is still openly acknowledged, is widely treated as the last problem to be solved by the invisible hand.

These days, apologetics take the form of promissory notes: "We are sorry that you're still poor, unemployed, sick, in debt, etc., but capital will get to you soon, so long as it's allowed to do its thing." But the existence of such apologetics can be taken as a good sign. Capitalism has got the upper hand, yet it still needs to justify itself at critical junctures in the face of its contradictions. The Occupy movements of 2011 and 2012 have shown this to be true, as they placed the word "capitalism" back into circulation in numerous countries that wanted to have done with the conversation decades ago. The Occupy movements gave rise

---

39   See Baudrillard, Jean, *For a Critique of the Political Economy of the Sign* (Telos, 1981) and *Symbolic Exchange and Death* (Sage Publications, 1993).

40   Marx, op. cit., p. 11.

to a new wave of apologetics that revealed the possibility for a defensive comportment on the part of capital. The offensive ones get defensive only when threatened.

When capital becomes a virtue, what is the fate of virtue? Virtue is always a normative consideration. It indicates a "noble" or "good" property of someone or something. Following the conversion of personal worth into exchange-value, virtue was rearranged thusly: If one is not paid for their work, their art, their books, their desires, such things have no value, and such things are therefore not as useful (in a society of monetary exchange relations) as those which have a value consummated by capital. In this way, capital determines both exchange-value and use-value. These terms were once separable, inasmuch as you could speak of diamonds (high exchange-value, low use-value) and water (low exchange-value, high use-value). But this is no longer true. If something has a low exchange-value, its use-value is ultimately undermined.

When John Locke wrote about the difference between perishable and durable property, he insisted that the former (perishable goods) should never be hoarded or wasted and that enough must be left for others in common, but the latter (durable goods) could be hoarded because things like diamonds and gold cannot be wasted, and are not necessary to human life.

> The greatest part of *things really useful* to the Life of Man, and such as the necessity of subsisting made the first Commoners of the World look after, as it doth the *Americans* now, *are* generally things *of short duration*; such as, if they are not consumed by use, will decay and perish of themselves: Gold, Silver and Diamonds, are things that Fancy or Agreement hath put the Value on, more than real Use, and the necessary Support of Life... He that *gathered* a Hundred Bushels of Acorns or Apples, had thereby a *Property* in them, they were his Goods as soon as gathered. He was only to look that he used them before they spoiled; else he took more than his share, and robb'd others... Again, if he would give us Nuts for a piece of Metal, pleased with its colour; or exchanged his Sheep for Shells, or Wool for a sparkling Pebble or a Diamond, and keep those by him all his Life, he invaded not

the Right of others, he might heap up as much of these
durable things as he pleased;[41]

When Locke philosophized about private property in the 17th century, he did not grasp that capital, and not labor, would become the
prerequisite for the acquisition of things necessary to human life. Locke
imagined exchange relations and private property acquisition in which
the worker was not expropriated from his working energies, and retained a natural right of ownership over the products of his labor. But
Locke also inadvertently established the rules for expropriation by clas-
sifying labor as a private property that could thus be sold to someone
else for a wage. The central normative issue is that, in the conflation of
use-value and exchange-value, and in the reduction of personal worth
to exchange-value, there was yet another sleight of hand, one which
renders capitalist value as virtue. Capitalist exchange relations smuggle
in a concept of right that automatically inscribes virtue into value, such
as when we say that someone "has done well," a phrase which contains
both senses of being (good) and having (money/property).

How far have we gone in reducing the value and virtue of all things
to capitalist exchange relations? There are at least two broad spheres
in which we can readily posit alter-values and alter-virtues to those
defined by capital. *alternative / logics .*

(1) We live in a world where exchange relations determine the life-
     activity of human societies. It is not possible to flee from capital-
     ism within a world governed by the operational logic of capital.
     John Holloway's *Crack Capitalism* is an important corrective to
     Hakim Bey's *T.A.Z. The Temporary Autonomous Zone.*[42] Holloway
     does not want to recommend temporary holidays from capital-
     ism. A fleeting zone of liberation only reaffirms the permanence
     of the opponent, as the T.A.Z. anticipates its end before it begins.
     Holloway thus prefers to envision cracks as fault lines that can
     grow, that will inevitably deepen and widen, creating opportuni-
     ties for us to recalibrate human relationality on a different logic

---

41   Locke, John, *Two Treatises of Government* (Cambridge University Press and Men-
     tor Books, 1965), Chapter 5, "Of Property," Section 46, p. 342.
42   Holloway, John, *Crack Capitalism* (Pluto Press, 2010), Bey, Hakim, *T.A.Z. The
     Temporary Autonomous Zone, Ontological Anarchy, Poetic Terrorism* (Autonome-
     dia, 2003).

than that of capitalist exchange relations. Holloway speaks of the community garden throughout *Crack Capitalism*, but not to suggest gardening as the antithesis to capitalism. His point is to illustrate other logics and possibilities for human association and activity than those of capital, and to highlight forms of association that are better, already practiced and practical, and sustainable.[43]

(2) The elusive contention that virtue is consummated by capital has been wearing out. People are less and less convinced that the most existentially meaningful things that they do are the things that they are paid to do, or pay to do. The virtue of capital is slowly being eclipsed by its regrettable inescapability. We continue to embrace capital and reproduce capitalism in our everyday lives, yet we do so because we must, not because we think it is virtuous. Capital has indeed attempted to convert all values and virtues into exchange-value, but we are unconvinced. We might wish to be paid for our music or artwork, but such works exist in spite of the total negation of their exchange-value. Activities that are not consummated by capital may well be leisurely, therapeutic, and lamentably infrequent, but we know their value well, and such activity cannot be disappeared by way of commoditization.

Capitalism continues to revolutionize production and exchange relations, but there is some evidence that it may be running out of ideas. For example, its apologists keep trying to resuscitate Ronald Reagan and Margaret Thatcher, to redeploy Adam Smith's invisible hand in surprisingly old ways, and Ayn Rand has re-entered mainstream public discourse in the US as a kind of visionary.

One of the biggest capitalist mythologies is that of endless new frontiers. Indeed, capitalism may be out of new frontiers. The thesis of endless new frontiers has always been deployed against Marx's crisis theory. Werner Sombart famously explored an answer to the question "Why is There No Socialism in the United States?" in 1906.[44] The title essay was written in the late 1800s, attesting to a history, which

---

43 See Holloway, John, *Crack Capitalism* (Pluto Press, 2010), pp. 4-5, for this and further examples of other modalities for human activity than those determined by the logic of capital.

44 Sombart, Werner, *Why is there no Socialism in the United States?* (M.E. Sharpe, 1976).

[handwritten top margin left: I think RGO wrong about finance capital ≠ it has been going since 17th century]

[handwritten top margin right: detour account of Marx's and new frontier scarcity]

- 34 -

[handwritten left margin: It is taking a PR hammering but is largely intact]

began shortly after Marx died, of capitalist societies outsmarting and outlasting every socialist antagonist on the horizon. But what is the next frontier for capitalism? We have since moved from industrial to informationalist and post-industrial capitalism, and we are well into a regime of finance capitalism in which money has been replaced with placeholders for money like credit, and financial instruments operate on the premise of real money being there somewhere down the line to substantiate, to back up, the whole system. The crisis of 2008-2012 was largely caused by real deficits of real money hiding underneath all the promises of financial placeholders, and revealed to many people in Greece and elsewhere throughout Europe and the US, that financial capitalism has been built on top of imaginary scaffolding.

[handwritten left margin: New frontiers being now planted? perhaps]

Marx was cautious about making predictions, as he was enamored by the revolutions of capital, marvelling over the fact that "fixed, fast-frozen relations, with their train of ancient and venerable prejudices and opinions, are swept away, all new-formed ones become antiquated before they can ossify."[45] Today, ossification and crisis stand in the way of the antiquation of finance capital, and the next new form is not yet visible. Marx famously wrote: "All that is solid melts into air, all that is holy is profaned, and man is at last compelled to face with sober senses his real conditions of life, and his relations with his kind."[46] But capital cannot melt everything down and create endless new horizons out of nothing.

[handwritten left margin: detour on flexibility of capital; RGO says its in trouble]

We can see the profanity of record profit margins amidst the generalized pain and precarity, but even the most ideological do not view such profit as "holy." We know this to be true from the Greek revolts and the Spanish Indignados, and from a severely, if not irreparably, damaged image of Wall Street. Over thirty years after the accelerated and unrivalled reign of neoliberal fantasies over human reality, capitalism seems to be the fantasy of a diminishing subset of the world population, whose fantasies mostly oppose existing conditions, as all good fantasies do.

[handwritten bottom margin: people are ever more conscious of capitals organisational logic]

(Internationalism and Its Discontents)

On the question of the globality of capitalism, Marx was remarkably prescient, critical, and precise. He knew well, already in the 1840s,

---

45 Marx, op. cit., p. 12.
46 Ibid.

that the growth and accumulation imperatives of capital would require obliterating the limitations of an already-mythical "national economy." We shall return to questions of globalization frequently throughout this book, in other sections than this one, but especially in Part IV.

The problems of globalization and the prospects for a cosmopolitan multitude reveal the greatest challenges of our time. It is difficult to imagine meeting these challenges. While capitalists have a rich history of transposing their whole apparatus into global networks, the *demos* still has a hard time substantiating democracy in national and sub-national contexts. The globality of capitalism has been growing and ongoing since Marx's life and times, and even in the context of the recent wave of uprisings, moments of contestation are fleeting. Cosmopolitanism can function as an ideal for revolutionaries, even for locally rooted movements focused on small autonomous action and community, because cosmopolitanism is ultimately a moral point of view that can be inhabited and practiced at any level of association. Capitalism has disfigured the cosmopolitan idea by way of the neoliberal contention that unbounded capital will eventually make everyone's life better. In their school, there is nothing left of Kant's conception of a hospitable "kingdom of ends," or of Habermas' conception of "cosmopolitan solidarity."[47] While capitalism deforms the Kantian and Habermasian cosmopolitan ideals, it at least makes use of its deformed vision. We, on the other hand, only preserve the good name of a cosmopolitan vision, but have not figured out how to make revolutionary use of it.

Michael Hardt and Antonio Negri are interested in the emergence of a revolutionary cosmopolitanism, even though they do not call themselves cosmopolitans. In response to the fierce demonstrations against the G-8 in Genoa, Italy in July of 2001, Hardt and Negri highlighted that the protesters "know that a fundamentally new global system is being formed. It can no longer be understood in terms of British, French, Russian or even American imperialism. The many protests that have led up to Genoa were based on the recognition that no national power is in control of the present global order... We are beginning to see emerge a multitude that is

Marginal notes: "Marx no concept of Nationalism ossifying the Further globulisation of capital" and "Another def own arent of both kant + Marx"

---

47   Kant, Immanuel, *Groundwork of the Metaphysics of Morals* (Cambridge University Press, 1998), p. 41; Habermas, Jürgen, *The Postnational Constellation: Political Essays* (The MIT Press, 2001), p. 112.

not defined by any single identity, but can discover commonality in its multiplicity."[48] It is indeed not necessary for communists to call themselves cosmopolitan, since Marx spent a lifetime of effort insisting upon internationalism against any national incarnation of his ideas, and even posits internationalism as a distinguishing feature of communism.[49] Typically, some form of cosmopolitanism or another characterizes the position of those who are critical of capitalist globalization today. And this is not always a Marxist position. Habermas' cosmopolitanism is far more Kantian than Marxist, and is essentially concerned with the prospects for a cosmopolitan EU that would reject its historic neoliberalism, but not capitalism itself. A similar position was outlined by Richard Falk, who argues for "globalization-from-below" in his book *Predatory Globalization: A Critique*.[50] Marx and Marxism have been ahead of the curve on the question of globalization, which is not, for communists in general, viewed as a new question to be raised only in the post-Cold War era. Marx rightly understood the notions of a "national proletariat" and a "national capitalist economy" as contradictions in terms.

Perhaps it is time that we throw this common communist principle into question without giving it up entirely. Perhaps, instead of looking for and looking forward to a globalized "antithesis" to capitalism in the world, we should take the implosion of capitalism's globality more seriously. After all, capitalism only has planet Earth (although Newt Gingrich wants to add the Moon as an American colony).[51] Our understanding of the limits of globalization has been largely enriched by the field of ecology. There is a long history of interest in globalizing an opposition to objectionable forms of globalization, but maybe going global is part of the problem. Crisis theory has been taken up in fruitful directions by eco-socialists, and has been given good articulation

---

48 Hardt, Michael and Negri, Antonio, "What the Protesters in Genoa Want" in *On Fire: The Battle of Genoa and the Anti-Capitalist Movement* (One-Off Press, 2001), pp. 101-103.

49 See especially Parts II and IV of *The Communist Manifesto* (International Publishers, 1994) and *Critique of the Gotha Programme* (International Publishers, 2002).

50 Falk, Richard, *Predatory Globalization: A Critique* (Polity Press, 1999), especially Chapter 8.

51 The joke disguises its seriousness. Space exploration is indeed a new horizon, and the vast untapped territories and resources of "outer space" are not lost on capital, which is more and more invested in realizing the fantasies of space travel.

[handwritten margin notes: Retournment of Mwk no global proletariat to organise just let people caused know of the global destruction of capital of by]

by James O'Connor.[52] The forward-looking "social ecology" of Murray Bookchin also points to certain limitations of growth and accumulation, and he has argued that globality will have to be scaled down, not so much as a choice but as a matter of ecological survival.[53] Others, like David Harvey, have expanded the thesis, arguing that capitalist globalization has a necessary expiration date to be determined when it reaches the limits of growth.[54] What one finds amongst these sources is an aggregate perspective that issues a kind of warning against following the global lead of capital. The classical empires of political history have issued similar warnings in their own ways. This view, then, which runs contrary to the positions of Kant, Marx, Habermas, Falk, and Hardt and Negri, suggests that we should not seek to address the problems of globalization by following its tendencies to scale-up, that we should not mirror its problematic logic of growth. Have some of the harshest critics of capitalist globalization, including Marx himself, emulated its most dangerous aspirations?

In light of the above considerations, and also, for anthropological and economic reasons, we must at least reject Marx's contention that bourgeois society "draws all nations, even the most barbarian, into civilization... it forces the barbarians' intensely obstinate hatred of foreigners to capitulate. It compels all nations, on pain of extinction, to adopt the bourgeois mode of production; it compels them to introduce what it calls civilization into their midst, i.e., to become bourgeois themselves. In one word, it creates a world after its own image."[55] This passage does better to catalogue the aspirations of capitalism than its actual historical achievements. Indeed, Marx understood the global division of labor well enough to know that capitalism could never civilize the so-called "barbarians," for capitalism depends on the preservation of "uncivilized barbarians" and does not even need to integrate every human person into the productive and consumptive systems that serve its interests. The "barbarian" remains necessary, and the barbaric treatment of people around the globe must continue, in order to support the polarized minority of capital's greatest beneficiaries, the

---

52   See, for example, O'Connor, James, *Natural Causes: Essays in Ecological Marxism* (The Guilford Press, 1998).

53   See Murray Bookchin's 1964 essay, "Ecology and Revolutionary Thought" in *The Murray Bookchin Reader* (Cassell, 1997), pp. 20-24.

54   See Harvey, David, *The Limits to Capital* (Verso, 2007).

55   Marx, op. cit., p. 13.

[handwritten margin note: Don't have global movements basically they could cause the same problems of capitalism]

least precarious among us. If capitalism ever achieved the total integration of the whole of humanity into its machinations, we would either have (a) too many proletarians or (b) too many bourgeoisie, which means either crisis-levels of unsolvable unemployment or not enough of an exploited class left over to make the clothes, cars, computers, not enough to grow the rice, pick up the garbage, clean up the hotel rooms, and populate the service sector. In actual fact, the tenuous trick of capitalism is to integrate just enough to avoid (a) or (b), and to lock populations of "barbarians" out as needed. It is therefore more accurate to say that capitalism seeks a world after its own spectacular image, so that while the "barbarian" is kept at bay, he sees himself (or is seen by others) as working himself out of an unfortunate position, however slowly. The ideology of upward mobility has been extrapolated into a global promise, which is in fact a lie. Those who have worked in the free trade zones of Jamaica, in the maquiladoras of Mexico, and in the rice farms of Honduras, Haiti, the Philippines and elsewhere, don't believe this lie as much as its perpetrators in the West.[56]

There is also a lie about the very globality of globalization. This is the lie that makes the world look as if everything is opened up to everyone, as if everything is available everywhere, as if power has been decentralized, as if all the monopolies of the 20th century have finally been broken up, and as if our technological capacity to digitalize democracy is spreading democracy everywhere. To this lie, scholars like Saskia Sassen should have dealt the final death blow many years ago, yet the basic mythology still survives. Sassen argued in two of her books, *Globalization and Its Discontents* and *Losing Control?* that beneath the image of globalization is a set of capitalist nerve centers, with actual physical locations, including physical infrastructures that are difficult to build and to move, and that are located in the wealthiest cities in the world for the interests of the wealthiest subsets of their populations.[57] Sassen wrote: "Much attention has gone to the new technologies' capacity for instantaneous transmission. But equally important is the extent to which the global financial markets are located

---

56   For a good expose of the Jamaican Free Trade Zones, see Stephanie Black's documentary *Life & Debt*, based on Jamaica Kincaid's book *A Small Place* (Farrar, Straus and Giroux, 2000).

57   Sassen, Saskia, *Globalization and Its Discontents: Essays on the New Mobility of People and Money* (New Press, 1999) and *Losing Control? Sovereignty in an Age of Globalization* (Columbia University Press, 1996).

in particular cities in highly developed countries. The degrees of con-
centration are unexpectedly high... What countries? Yes, the usual
suspects: the United States, the U.K., Japan, Switzerland, France,
Germany, and Luxembourg."[58] The globality of globalization is, therefore, at least a little misleading given that its organizational centers
are anchored to a small number of geographic locations, and given
that the same cities remain the integral sites for the accumulation of
capital. All of this is critical to keep in mind given that the concept of
"globalization" often takes on a metaphysical connotation, obscuring
its material physicality.

What this means is that increasing globalization does not necessarily undermine existing relations of political-economic power. Part of
the efficacy of capitalist globalization involves a confounding ideology
of internationalism that globalization itself betrays in practice.

We see then: capitalism is earthly, drawing upon earthly human
and non-human resources, and yet has not ceased to extract, exploit,
control, and to exhaust (in some cases) such resources. Human resources continue to grow, but with them so too do human needs,
while the non-human resources on which earthly life depends are not
so easy to reproduce. While ecologists speak of "non-renewable" resources, the logic of capital stubbornly resists, seeing instead perpetual
opportunities for accumulation and growth, even looking at technological efforts to replace non-renewable resources as potentially good
news. When Marx wrote about the working and exchange relations of
feudal societies, he saw the limitations from the perspective of capital,
and he concluded that the arrangements of feudalism "had to be burst
asunder; they were burst asunder."[59] We are not at the end of history,
for there is more still to be burst asunder.

Today, all of the surrogates of capital rail against state power, the
latter of which has virtually volunteered its irrelevance by handing
over its specific functions to the private sector. But there is still more
"capitalist freedom" to be sought that could burst asunder the last
bastions of welfarist commitments as, for example, austerity measures
throughout Europe make a clear itemization of every provision that
needs to go. Capital and its surrogates will always have a gripe until
the total freedom of capital is achieved, where freedom is defined only
in reference to the mobility of capital. Capital and its surrogates, who

---

58   Sassen, Saskia, *Losing Control?* (Columbia University Press, 1996), pp. 12-13.
59   Marx, op. cit., p. 14.

are also its apologists, would prefer a legal system that applies no laws to the regulation of capital in the purported interest of finally being able to prove its self-correcting powers to make everyone prosperous according to its own laws. In this regard, there are still some roles of the state that capital wants to burst asunder.

(Freedom and Mystification, Mystification of Freedom)

But on the other side of all this is another interest in a different kind of bursting asunder. The purely ideological and brazenly self-serving definition of freedom according to capital must be burst asunder by another conception of freedom – *of autonomy* – a conception of freedom more robustly defined for the autonomy of everyday people, which invokes *our* mobility – not the mobility of capital – *our* ability to stretch ourselves out toward what we desire to be, to do, to become. Such a freedom as this must be counterposed to the false freedoms of the neoliberal faith. An autonomist perspective does not choose between state and market, because it understands the collaborationist history of those two sides and sees well that neither one of them on their own would guarantee anything anyway. Autonomist politics involves rethinking freedom in the grey areas, in between and against the typical dichotomies of power. It is necessary to be more precise.

What, exactly, is meant by autonomist theory, autonomist politics, and autonomist Marxism? While a fuller and more focused discussion appears in Part III, Section 1, *B.*, I shall provide some working definitions here. First of all, we generally avoid the term "autonomism" for the same reasons that Debord rejected the term "situationism."[60] We do not want to indicate any comprehensive worldview, and do not want to adopt the linguistic form that specifies an ideology, which we oppose as a matter of principle. "Autonomist," therefore, much like "situationist," indicates an approach, or rather, an approach to various approaches in theory and practice. Wherever we use "ism" as a matter of expediency and clarity in conversation, we try to differentiate the philosophical from the ideological form (the spectacle form), as in communism versus "communism," respectively.

---

60   See, for one example, Debord, Guy, *Considerations on the Assassination of Gérard Lebovici* (TamTam Books, 2001), p. 73.

Autonomist Marxists are not interested in alternative or "radical" lifestyles, or in fixating on the individual as an asocial entity, but autonomist Marxists do give these "smaller" spheres of life more serious consideration than conventional Marxists do, for the latter insist upon macrosocial, structural, class analysis as a defining and enduring primary commitment. Autonomist Marxists also engage in class analysis, for we live, think, and work in class societies and thus cannot dispense with macrosocial and structural modes of critique – but we mix it up as needed, we question the veracity of class analysis at every juncture, and we do so freely and honestly without any sense of betrayal.

Primarily, the autonomy of autonomist approaches refers, in the first place, to a "freedom from" the official parties, institutions, and representatives of the Left – including labor unions – and all of their general and particular directives. This means that whenever autonomist positions line up with the initiatives of the official Left, it is only happenstance or temporary, and never to be counted on. It is even possible that, when the right-wing calls for states to allow dying capitalist institutions to collapse, such as banks and auto companies, an autonomist may well second the call, although for completely different reasons. In the second place, the autonomy of autonomist approaches refers to a "freedom to" act creatively and even sporadically beyond or even against the agendas of the official Left. True, this freedom warmly (and consciously) invites individuals to consider their personal talents, desires, and proclivities when determining various modalities of political involvement, and hopefully, this freedom leads to surprise, to new aesthetic approaches, and to autonomous actions that are impossible to target by opponents looking for the central nervous system of our rhizomatic efforts. But autonomist politics does not rule out collective action, and by no means do we ever exaggerate the significance of any isolated upheaval or expression of disaffection and desire. On the other hand, wildcat or general strikes or mass actions like those in Paris in 1968, in Seattle in 1999, in Genoa in 2001, or in Oakland, CA in 2011, may well advance a class analysis by way of collective action while remaining fully autonomous in the sense defined above. That is, these collective actions may be large and even highly coordinated or organized, and at the same time they may be fully beyond the control of political parties and unions, and they may have no cohesive agenda, despite the best efforts of some of the participants to establish one. Autonomous expressions of disaffection can

analyse individual expressions in collective realms

be unpredictable, spontaneous, and dangerous, which is what makes them both effective and affective. Within this context, the term "singularity" does not connote the individual person, but rather, singular expressions of disaffection and desire that may or may not link up with other such singularities in a unified way.

In one of the most important passages in *The Communist Manifesto*, Marx writes: "Modern bourgeois society, with its relations of production, of exchange and of property, a society that has conjured up such gigantic means of production and of exchange, is like the sorcerer who is no longer able to control the powers of the nether world whom he has called up by his spells."[61] This might have been in the minds of Gilles Deleuze and Félix Guattari when they declared: "Capital is indeed the body without organs of the capitalist, or rather of the capitalist being."[62] Sorcery is also the subject of the book *Capitalist Sorcery: Breaking the Spell* by Phillipe Pignarre and Isabelle Stengers, who consider a politics of "counter-magic."[63] Indeed, the question of magic and the image of the sorcerer deserve some closer consideration.

The magician produces illusions by sleights of hand, deceptions, and other techniques. The honest magician operates on the premise of crafting illusions, of entertainment, and does not claim to be exercising supernatural powers. A good magician even encourages your specific bewilderment about trying to figure out how the trick has been done. A good magician could have you wracking your brain, astonished at the mastery of the trick, even wondering about how what you have seen is possible as an illusion. That is the good work of the magician. Sorcery, though, has a different connotation, for sorcery evokes the aid of spirits, the supernatural, and witchery. In this regard, it is perhaps better to speak of capitalist magic than of capitalist sorcery, especially today when there is a kind of honesty about political-economic sleights of hand and deceptions (i.e., tax and trade policies, structural adjustment programs, austerity measures). Bluntly put, is there anyone who is either (a) surprised that the everyday functioning of capitalism rests on the tricks of masters, or (b) believes that existing relations of wealth and poverty embody and reflect a supernatural

---

61   Marx, op. cit., p. 14.
62   Deleuze, Gilles and Guattari, Félix, *Anti-Oedipus: Capitalism and Schizophrenia* (Penguin Books, 2009), p. 10.
63   See Pignarre, Philippe and Stengers, Isabelle, *Capitalist Sorcery: Breaking the Spell* (Palgrave Macmillan, 2011).

order of things? We know that capital is accumulated on Wall Street, or by investors and hedge fund managers by way of certain tricks, even if we don't know how such tricks are performed. We know that upward mobility and fairness are more illusion than they are the actual facts of macroeconomic and macrosocial realities. And we hardly think, or would admit in public, that what we own reflects the moral worth of what we do and who we are.

Nonetheless, the unabashed ruthlessness of capital has not killed magic or sorcery. With magic, the entertainment value of watching capitalist sleights of hand, without always understanding how capital accumulates, has made it into an acceptable trickery of the system for so many precarious people. And with sorcery, there still lurks a supernatural thesis about God's plan, which gives our acceptance of the existing state of affairs a cosmic justification. These elements are still present, even if they are no longer necessary, or overdetermining of the situation.

When Marx wrote of sorcery beyond the control of the sorcerer, he sought to illustrate the inevitability of capitalist crises that come from unleashing forces beyond even the capitalist's control. In other words, this example was part of Marx's conversation on crisis theory. In the paragraph where Marx speaks of sorcery, he speaks also of systemic crisis, that the "conditions of bourgeois society are too narrow to comprise the wealth created by them. And how does the bourgeoisie get over these crises?"[64] To his question, Marx offers two answers. First, he says that the defenders of the existing system can create more tenuous conditions to further oblige working people to obey the logic of capital. Second, Marx offers that by seizing new markets elsewhere, and by further exploiting existing markets, capitalists could defer, displace, or postpone crisis.

Marx did not explicate the third way that capital survives its own crises, for the third way was only developed more resolutely in the twentieth-century wake of Sigmund Freud, Wilhelm Reich, and psychoanalysis, characteristically taken up as the cause of the critical theorists of Germany and France. We now know this third way well vis-à-vis the many ways that capitalism prevents people from seeing capitalist crisis as having anything to do with capitalism, its logic, or its culture. This third possibility, which Marx grasped in a prototypical

---

64   Marx, op. cit., p. 15.

way in his discussion of apologetics, became an art-form in the 20th century. In light of this, the weapons with which the bourgeoisie felled feudalism cannot be so easily turned against the "bourgeoisie" of today. Those old weapons are not the ones we have inherited. Crisis still matters, for crises change the opportunity structure for political action. But, contrary to Marx's revolutionary optimism, no crisis is guaranteed, and even if one crisis or another were clearly visible on the horizon, such crisis guarantees nothing to the antagonists of capital. This uncertainty, this lack of any revolutionary confidence, is part of what makes communism all the more precarious today.

(Class Analysis and the Calling of the Precariat?)

Marx already recognized what is today called "precarity," he perhaps defined it better than anyone since, and theories of precarity owe much to his formulation, which should remain a touchstone. Marx defined the proletariat as "those who live only so long as they find work, and who find work only so long as their labor increases capital. These laborers, who must sell themselves piecemeal, are a commodity, like every other article of commerce, and are consequently exposed to all the vicissitudes of competition, to all the fluctuations of the market."[65] The only promise of our precarity is that there will be no promises, no commitments, besides those that we might make in love, with family, friends, partners, or children. Aside from such personal exceptions, the promise of no promises is what governs the broader spheres of society, politics, and economics.

We know that the interests of profit will always trump any of capital's weak and ephemeral commitments to us, which is partly why contracts are necessary. This is also why unions still serve a purpose inasmuch as they aim to regulate the precarity of labor and to provide at least a modicum of reassurance. The "outsourcing" and "downsizing" of the 1980s and 1990s have liquidated any meaningful sense of commitment. But there's some good news, for this very problem has a dangerous double. Workers everywhere find less and less nobility in the so-called "virtue" of hard work, for they return to capital the favor

65   Ibid.

of making no promises, as workers today show no enduring commitments to their employers. If capital makes no commitments to the everyday people who make it possible, capital can expect no commitments from us. Like the so-called free market, we can be unpredictable too, in many different ways. This becomes clear when we think about the most famous bad word of the capitalist workplace, "insubordination," whose supposedly noble opposite is the less celebrated word, "subordination."

The standardized form of repetitive factory work turned out to be more flexible than it looked in the 19th century, even largely replaceable. In response to the old, industrial models of standardization, the second half of the 20th century introduced an ever-growing level of "personalization" into the monotonous contexts of everyday life. But this is a peculiar personalization that can be achieved wholly within the limits of standardization. Consider, once again, the example of the mass exodus from MySpace to Facebook. Facebook allows for personalization within the limits of standardization, whereas MySpace suffered in part from insufficient standardization. Consider the trends of altered work spaces, computer desktop layouts, cell phone settings, ringtones and playlists, carrying cases and protective sleeves, in addition to the usual suspects, i.e., lifestyle magazines for every rebellious type, for those with a pseudo-situationist flare who can purchase *AdBusters* in a Whole Foods Market checkout line. Indeed, personalization enters the capitalist workplace on the same premises that *AdBusters* enters the grocery store, because of a final confirmation that mass-marketed expressions of individuality pose no threat to capital, but instead, give it a noble gloss. The rerouting of Marx here perhaps feels as old as Theodor Adorno and Max Horkheimer's commentary on standardized individuality in the "Culture Industry" chapter of *Dialectic of Enlightenment*.[66] But there is at least one important difference. The standardized individuality of the culture industry no longer functions in the elusive ways of the 1940s and 50s. That is, we are no longer dealing with false consciousness as much as a self-conscious irony, which we knowingly accept. For example, the irony of buying *AdBusters* in a grocery store cannot be lost on an avid reader of that publication, for the publication points out the irony in its own pages. More broadly, no one really thinks that their personality is actually

---

66   See Adorno and Horkheimer, "The Culture Industry: Enlightenment as Mass Deception" in *Dialectic of Enlightenment* (Continuum, 1997).

embodied and reflected in the settings of their technological devices. Increasingly, on the terrain of consumption, one's taste is just one's taste, on the level of a banal preference, and not a serious declaration of personal identity.[67]

This may or may not be good news. It is not good news if the culture industry no longer needs to make use of the "false consciousness" of desire and identity. What if we no longer care about the question of "authenticity" in the ways it was raised in the 1940s, the time of *Dialectic of Enlightenment*, the decade in which Jean-Paul Sartre's *Being and Nothingness* opened up the French existentialist movement? As a movement of any kind, existentialism is long dead and buried, and for many different reasons. The erosion of real interest in the authenticity of being may be one such reason. In the critical theory of Germany and France, a philosophical discourse on authenticity had emerged, but perhaps today no one bemoans, or even worries, about the loss of authenticity. On the other hand, our ability to plainly see the irony of personalization as a feature of an otherwise standardized life undermines the functional necessity of false consciousness. Maybe now we can see these contradictions in a more immediate way. But none of these changes, inasmuch as they could even be measured, bring about the gratification of our desires. Personalization of the workplace does not reverse the repulsiveness of work. Repulsion is not being mitigated by pay raises. What is the good news? We are perhaps closer to confronting the repulsiveness of work in the light of its open contradictions.

Adorno and Horkheimer's discussions of work in *Towards a New Manifesto* provide a more enduring analysis of a more enduring problem than the problems of mass deception and the culture industry. In that conversation, Horkheimer asserts that "freedom means not having to work," to which Adorno replies: "Philosophy always asserts that freedom is when you can choose your own work, when you can claim ownership of everything awful."[68] The point is crucial. It remains a

---

67   I do not deny that class and cultural identities are still embodied and announced in the personal ownership of certain products, i.e., cars, clothing, technological devices. This can be seen in the common example of the social status of Apple technology. But such cachet has been wearing out since the proliferation of other "preferences" that are not so different anymore, and the choice to carry one phone over another mostly indicates some sensible and banal decision, within the normal range of expectations (including the expectation that you have one).

68   Adorno, Theodor and Horkheimer, Max, *Towards a New Manifesto* (Verso, 2011), p. 16.

defining part of the capitalist mythology that, if one chooses work that they hate to do, the choice attests to their freedom nonetheless. Later in the conversation, Adorno continues the argument: "Self-determination means that within the division of labour already laid down I can slip into the sector that promises me the greatest rewards." Horkheimer adds: "The idea that freedom consists in self-determination is really rather pathetic, if all it means is that the work my master formally ordered me to do is the same as the work I now seek to carry out of my own free will."[69] If freedom is to be defined as some form of self-determination, then it cannot be self-determination within the limits of capital. We shall work out a conception of autonomy that exceeds the "pathetic" limitations sharply pointed out by Adorno and Horkheimer later on in this book, specifically in Part III, Section 1, B. But one of our overarching goals must indeed be to deal with that false opposition noted by Horkheimer in his observation that "the opposite of work is regarded as nothing more than consumption."[70] We must think through other spheres of autonomy than those available between working and shopping.

Marx's description of work has in many cases been clearly outstripped: "Masses of laborers, crowded into the factory, are organized like soldiers. As privates of the industrial army they are placed under the command of a perfect hierarchy of officers and sergeants."[71] Marx could not foresee the post-industrial revolutions made by capitalists who realized that an unregimented, non-hierarchical and networked form of capitalism could be developed without threatening the dominance of the logic of capital at all, without threatening the consolidation of capitalist power. Google, Pixar, and Facebook are companies well-known for modelling so-called workplace liberation, which despite these companies' retention of hierarchical infrastructure, "free up" the constraints depicted in Marx's military analogy. Increasingly, as capital lauds the productivity and profitability of these new models, we will see more and more people working in open spaces that look and feel like avant-garde cafés, like hipster artist warehouses, to personalize, or perhaps to disguise, the capitalist workplace so that it no longer bears any resemblance to that standardized industrial setting Marx likened to boot camp.

---

69 Ibid., pp. 24-25.
70 Ibid., p. 26.
71 Marx, op. cit., p. 16.

[handwritten margin note: liberating work (in this epoch) is personalized or disguised work. No longer looks like industrial setting]

Beyond all of this, the old models of discipline, now including Michel Foucault's discussion of the panoptic tower, have ended up not being as vital to the interests of capital as has been thought.[72] In Foucault's analysis, for example, biopower shifts control from the brute forces of repression to a more elusive psycho-social force. Yet, with panoptic control, surveillance is still something that is done to us by others in order to keep us in line. There must first be a gaze to interiorize. But today, we happily and voluntarily place ourselves under surveillance and even feel snubbed when we cannot command the attention of the gaze of others. For Foucault, the guard could leave the central tower, and those of us living in the cells would never know if the tower was occupied and active and so would behave as if it were. Today, the tower can also go away with the guard. We set up our own towers everywhere. Everything that the eye of power could see by way of surveillance, through panoptic technology, is now given up freely to the world in tweets, global positioning systems, reality television, and of course, social media.

Critics have pointed to Marx's supposed failure to account for the re-emergence of the middle class. Critics note that Marx only saw the world as splitting up into two hostile camps, while the 20th century reintroduced a growing middle class that effectively softened the antagonisms between the bourgeoisie and proletariat. Marx did write of the middle class in *The Communist Manifesto*, acknowledging their important historical existence in many places, but nonetheless held that they would "sink gradually into the proletariat."[73] Something must be said about both the critical claims levelled against Marx, and Marx's own contention. Both sides – the claim that the middle class has re-emerged as well as Marx's claim that it would disappear – are imprecise.

Evidence supporting the figure of the re-emerged middle class can be found in constant political discourse about it. Every politician in the US, for example, addresses him or herself to the middle class, and knows well that he or she must speak about what will be best for the middle class, for the largest, the hardest working, tax-paying class, for the class for whom policies really matter most, and thus, for the class that turns out votes in the greatest numbers. If there was no such

72   See Foucault, *Discipline and Punish* (Vintage Books, 1995) and *Power/Knowledge* (Pantheon Books, 1980).

73   Marx, op. cit., p. 17.

thing as a massive middle class today, how could it end up being the meaningful subject of so many political speeches? Before addressing this question, we should note that it is true that the re-emergence of a burgeoning middle class would indeed be a problem for Marx, since the dialectical content of historical materialism consists largely in the growing antagonism of the classes, an antagonism that would be mitigated by an intermediary class to buffer the conflict. The nature of this challenge to class analysis is important to comprehend. If the most impoverished among us can find an image of their future in the middle class, even if they only climb into the lowest ranks of that class (the "lower middle class"), then they could deal with their class disadvantage through upward mobility. Thus, the image of the middle class presents a promise within reach to poor people, which puts those on the bottom close enough to the middle to pre-empt radical measures. If, as Marx predicted, the proletariat could only see the bourgeoisie from afar, the great and growing distance between them would eventually recommend more radical measures, and ultimately, revolution. But such measures appear superfluous when the distance between the bottom and the middle is perceived to be small enough to make the journey. At the same time, if the top is perpetually aware of its proximity to the middle, and cognizant of the possibility that it could slip into the middle class by way of unforeseen crisis, then those on the top might see the welfare of those in the middle as part of their own self-interest. Hence, the viability of this suggestion, of the idea of a large and growing middle class, effectively reconciles a good deal of the affective antagonisms between the top and the bottom. In this way, the re-emergence of a middle class would indeed undermine Marx's theory of revolutionary class conflict.

However, the criticism I've outlined above neglects overwhelming evidence from noncontroversial and mainstream sources that refute the claims of upward mobility and substantiate the reality of growing inequality everywhere. According to the neoliberal Organization for Economic Cooperation and Development (OECD) in 2011, of the 34 countries in the group, the US has greater income inequality than any country besides Turkey, Chile, and Mexico. The UK, with its aggressive neoliberalism and privatization initiatives from the 1970s on, is also one of the countries toward the bottom of the list. The greatest amount of income equality – or the smallest gaps between rich and poor – is to be found in Slovenia, the Slovak Republic, Denmark, and

Norway. The data ranks countries by the Gini Coefficient, making it fairly good data (as far as such data goes), and certainly very conservative in its estimates. Within the US alone, from 1979 to 2003, the poorest subset of the population (measured by income level) saw their average real income increase by only one hundred to a few thousand dollars over the course of that 24-year period. By comparison, over the same 24 years (1979 to 2003), the average real income of the wealthiest 1% grew by well over half a million dollars, and the top 5-10% also saw major growth.[74]

There are other measures than income. In 2006, the United Nations Development Programme (UNDP) identified global access to water as the defining crisis of the 21st century. Yet, this is still related to capital because "there is more than enough water in the world... The problem is that the poor are systematically excluded from access by their poverty... In short, scarcity is manufactured through political processes and institutions that disadvantage the poor."[75] The 2012 UNDP report, Africa Human Development Report 2012: *Towards a Food Secure Future* highlights "food security" as catastrophic for millions starving and dying in sub-Saharan Africa. But, as with water access, this food security crisis must not be allowed to obscure the facts of its direct relationship to capital: "Developed countries maintain agricultural subsidies that benefit their rich producers while pushing sub-Saharan Africa's impoverished smallholder farmers to the margins. For many years externally inspired adjustment programmes weakened state capacity and encouraged African governments to repay ballooning debts by diverting resources from food production to cash crop exports. One by one countries fell victim to falling commodity prices and increasingly volatile and costly imports."[76]

The logic of capital scarcely bothers to hide behind these noncontroversial facts of growing inequality, of manufactured scarcity, and of the command of the world's natural and agricultural resources. Indeed, the competitive proprietary interests of capital, and the associated pathologies of accumulation and growth, are the only sensible

---

74 Economic Policy Institute, *The State of Working America 2006/2007* (Cornell University Press, 2007).
75 Human Development Report 2006: *Beyond Scarcity: Power, Poverty and the Global Water Crisis* (Palgrave Macmillan, 2006), p. 3.
76 Africa Human Development Report 2012: *Towards a Food Secure Future* (United Nations Publications, 2012), p. vi.

explanations we have left, after ruling out racist caricatures, the myth of upward mobility, and the sham of scarcity. Ideology imposes numerous screens that obscure our view of the basic facts of human suffering, but these particular features (the ones discussed here, at least) are plain to see for those willing to look.

Following this, and in the light of any fairly good macroeconomic picture, what kind of real "hope" does the middle class offer to the poor, and what kind of real "threat" is it for the wealthiest among us that they might fall into the middle class? Who is in the middle class and who is not? When the Economic Policy Institute measures income growth and equality in the US, they distinguish the levels as "bottom," "second," "middle," "fourth," "top 80th - <95th percentile," and the "top five percent."[77] Looking at income by fifths or sixths yields a more precise picture of meaningful and measurable differences within class stratifications, yet political discourses continue to float above such distinctions invoking a potentially-all-inclusive middle class. In contrast to the actual facts of macroeconomic stratification, there is the peculiar phenomenon that most people are capable of seeing themselves as part of the middle class, or as its future members. The reality and resonance of this perception explains why political speeches always address the middle class.

Let us consider the middle class as an illusory community. *let our own*

How many extremely wealthy people see themselves as "upper middle class," and how seriously should we take those self-identifications? According to the Economic Policy Institute in 2012, those in top 80th - <95th percentile have an average family income of 150,016 USD. Yet these people, who are not even close to the socioeconomic position of middle family incomes (the middle has an average family income of 62,268 USD) commonly see themselves as in the middle class, and not even necessarily in the upper of the middle class. The top five percent makes an average family income of 323,183 USD, and not even that is enough to convince such people of their distance from the "real" middle.[78] For many in the top five percent (who are in fact not very many), as long as you can't see glaring indicators of their wealth, and as long as they can point to others who have more, they will call themselves "middle class" without further qualification.

77   See *The State of Working America: 12th Edition* (Cornell University Press, 2012), Chapter 2, Table 2.1, p. 59.
78   Ibid.

On the other side, how many poor people have adopted the language of calling themselves "lower middle class," by which they can imagine themselves climbing just a bit, ever closer toward the middle of that middle? Living on credit with debt is a major part of the middle class sensibility of the poor. The poor can live on credit with debt as if they're not poor, with many of the same features and experiences of a "rich" life, within the limits of credit and for a particular time being. When we consult our own colloquial self-understandings, therefore, the top is in the middle and the bottom is in the middle too.

The rationale of this deceptive discourse can be explained: "Bourgeois" functions as an insult to liberals and conservatives alike, and there is no doubt that Mitt Romney's extreme wealth irreparably damaged his image amongst working class people across ideological divides in the 2012 election. While no one wants to really be seen as "bourgeois," no one wants to be poor either. The appeal of the middle class makes perfect sense on an affective level. In this way, rather than every class disappearing into the proletariat or the bourgeoisie, as Marx foresaw, the proletariat and the bourgeoisie have "disappeared" into the middle class, but the middle class into which they have disappeared doesn't even exist.

The first side of the story, the side according to which the middle class has *really* re-emerged, is falsified by the second story, according to which it *really* has not. But the second side of the story, according to which the re-emergence of the middle class is a fantasy that betrays macroeconomic reality, is without great consequence because the strength of that fantasy has effectively pre-empted the development of a critical class analysis. Broadly speaking, there are still two classes, although they have evolved beyond the definitions of the proletariat and the bourgeoisie. We could say that there are those who live in a world of their own making (more or less) who can more confidently determine their own future, and then there are those who live in a world of someone else's making who have no reassurances of any future in particular. At bottom, class is about self-determination in the more robust sense of being-in-the-world, which includes being able to determine the course of one's life. The first class, the less precarious, still includes precious few. The second class, the more precarious, includes most of the world's population. And the second class is not only determined economically, but also socially, for it contains those of despised sexualities, marginalized "racial" and other communities, indigenous populations under the attack of free trade agreements, refugees, fugitives, artists and other precarious people, with all of their bivalent compositions and intersectionalities.

The middle class as an illusory community is a problem for Marxism today. Members of the differentiated social groups we have been discussing, whether distinguished by fifths or sixths of income or by sexual identity, have too easily come to see themselves as living in "the middle," despite their other differences, and therefore feel close enough to this great and growing middle to render any radical proposal an "irrational" choice when compared to the promise of hard work. To be sure, the fantasy of the middle class is a neoliberal fantasy. Nonetheless, while the fantastic middle class does not exist in fact, it functions biopolitically as a dream or a nightmare that inhibits so many insurrectionary aspirations from taking root.

The hope of dialectical thinking is that the most precarious among us, the "precariat," shall go through various stages of development. A deepening and widening recognition of the total insecurity and uncertainty of capitalism's promise gives birth to the precarious class. This means that the precariat does not come about in purely materialist ways. Its emergence depends upon realizations of material insecurity that are difficult to achieve because of intervening ideologies, including those of upward mobility and the middle class. But every mythology has an expiration date and ideology is capable of wearing out. Debord was correct when he declared: "Stretched to its absolute limit, ideology *disintegrates*: its supreme form is also its absolute zero: the night where all ideological cows are black... The joyous end of ideological lies, struck dead by ridicule, is at hand."[79] Here, Debord was speaking about the ideology that wanted to obscure the catastrophes of the so-called communist world as well as the fact that the so-called communist world was not communist at all. Debord argued against the Cold War contention that "communist" regimes were making communism happen in "our world at large."[80] For Debord, this was one of the central ideologies in the process of disintegrating, having largely revealed itself as a lie by 1967. Today, we are seeing the slow disintegration of capitalist ideologies. Yet, the precariat is not overwhelmingly directing its disaffection at capitalism as the rotten operational logic of the world. At first, the precariat asks for – before

79   Debord, *A Sick Planet* (Seagull Books, 2008), pp. 72-73.
80   Ibid., p. 73.

it demands – the security that it does not have; at first, the precariat wants capitalism to make good on its impossible promises. But is there a dialectical development on the horizon where the precarious people of the world will see the impracticality of capitalism and stop paying and praying for its ongoing salvation?

People are more mobile and privatized than ever before, while our unhinged individuation is made coherent by the "social" façade of new media. What is a "compact body" today? What is an "active union?" The privatization of social life makes it difficult to predict historic feats of collective action, and bluntly, impossible to plan them.[81] No person, no compact body, and no active union can make a revolution by plans and agendas today. It is questionable whether that was ever possible. But the crises of the present state of affairs remain capable of setting large parts of the precariat into motion, which could be seen in moments of revolt, occupations, and even (if not especially) in riots. In moments of upheaval throughout the civil societies of the world, the precarious do not necessarily confront their enemies directly, but they do make collective expressions of disaffection against everyday life, about their anxiety over the prospects for any desirable "future." Upheavals of the precariat, specific cases of which we shall discuss throughout this book, express a rejection of the system's own channels for registering their unhappiness. But the historical movement against, through, and beyond capitalism is not concentrated into the hands of anyone in particular, or of any compact body or active union, and is thus a movement that, despite (*or because of*) its fragmentary uncertainty, cannot be imprisoned, executed, or permanently pre-empted.

It is difficult to assess the quality and quantity of powers that the precarious of the world might wield. We often only discover capabilities after they're realized in action. We do know that the wealthiest and least precarious, that tiny faction of, say, the richest 5% of people on the planet, have a security that is contingent upon what Fredy Perlman called the reproduction of daily life.[82] Perlman argues that everything remaining more or less as it is in the world, including existing stratifications and power relations, depends upon everyday people continuing to reproduce daily life as it is. But our grievances

---

81   See Habermas, Jürgen, *Legitimation Crisis* (Beacon Press, 1975), for what remains one of the best discussions of the privatization of social life.

82   Perlman, Fredy, "The Reproduction of Everyday Life" in *Anything Can Happen* (Phoenix Press, 1992).

are more multifarious than ever. The interests and conditions of life within the ranks of the precariat are diversified in so many directions, and so many different consumption patterns absorb the different frustrations. When enough people come to share the same grievance, they constitute a viable market from the perspective of capital. The fragmentary diversification of the precariat runs contrary to Marx's contention of increasing standardization and the levelling out of all other differences than class. As mentioned, however, Marx explicitly foresaw the emergence of the precariat. "The unceasing improvement of machinery, ever more rapidly developing, makes their livelihood more and more precarious."[83]

The key difference between Marx's sense of precarity and the present sense is that precariousness is no longer driven by the technological developments of the machinery of production. While technology continues to play a critical role, as we have discussed, for example, in the new mind-body split and the cellular format for time, it is the increasing fluidity and mobility of capital that accounts for the increasing precarity of everyday life. In other words, capital can come and go quickly, by surprise, and beyond the command of expert capitalists who may also find themselves tossed about by the unpredictable waves of a crisis they didn't see coming.[84] Previously, workers saw unions as a hopeful means for uniting against the bourgeoisie; today, workers seek unions as a desperate means for securing ever-diminishing returns. Workers today widely understand unions as worth fighting for only inasmuch as they do damage control on the growing precarity of work and capital.

Ever since 1848, whenever the working class was victorious, in a strange way, so was capitalism. The victories of the workers were also victories for capital, but this was not immediately clear, and only visible from the longer retrospective of history. Capitalism has never been mortally wounded by oppositional forces, for whenever it has been pushed around by external demands it has demonstrated an eventual compatibility with such demands. This can be illustrated in

---

83 Marx, op. cit., p. 18.

84 Of course, capitalists also have a long history of planning and profiting from economic crisis. As capitalists, however, their apologetics prevent them from seeing systems-crises intrinsic to capitalism and its logic. Rather, for the capitalist, crisis is always the result of particular moves made by individual players. Moreover, from their point of view, crisis is only acknowledged on the level of economy and is regarded as a change in the opportunity structure for investment.

our discussion of unions. Everywhere in the world, unions are less and less consciously or openly anticapitalist. Unions have been efficiently integrated into capitalism, to varying degrees in different countries, or else they are powerless and non-existent. That is, unions only retain their limited powers as a result of their general agreement with and actual integration into capitalism, at which point they even function as a component of the legitimation of capitalism. Marx had little faith in trade unions for many of the same reasons, although he hoped they would inadvertently contribute to the historical production of an expanding class of revolutionary workers. Contrary to this aspiration, trade unions have not developed in that direction and have mostly travelled down an opposite path. As a vehicle for worker demands against capital, unions have also functioned to soften antagonisms between workers and their employers, to help make nice wherever ugliness is stirring. At certain points throughout the 20th century a sensible Marxist could have concluded that, without the ameliorations of trade unions, disgruntled workers might have turned revolutionary. Marxists have long been concerned about unionism as a pill that makes the miserable more bearable. Indeed, one could argue that when unions work well, that is exactly what they do, they prevent revolutionary disaffections from growing.

It is easy to point out today that Marx was too optimistic about revolution. Speaking of the proletariat engaged in its historic struggle, he said that "it ever rises up again, stronger, firmer, mightier."[85] That those forced down ever rise again is the vital truth of dialectics and we could indeed provide much supportive evidence for the claim. However, the accumulating and consolidating strength, firmness, and might of the working class is either accruing with imperceptible slowness, or has been absorbed and defeated in various ways unpredicted by Marx. The latter reflects my own contention.

Who are the most likely enemies of the most influential, wealthiest, and least precarious among us? This old question is not as easy to answer today as it was for Marx, for we cannot simply name (or rename) the exploited, disaffected class. We live in class societies, but are rarely involved in battles with one another drawn sharply along class lines. Moreover, human history is not always the history of battles or conflicts and, even though we cannot be categorical pacifists,

---

85   Marx, op. cit., p. 18.

speaking of human history in only such terms gives too much credit to struggle. History is also full of feats of cooperation and voluntary kindness, periods of mystification, subordination, and plenty of "off stage" disaffection, as James C. Scott has shown in his *Domination and the Arts of Resistance*. Indeed, Scott understands that much of history is written in unreadable spaces, on the hidden transcript of the exploited and disaffected, and that the major historic moments made in open acts of defiance have long invisible histories.[86] Marx insisted that the bourgeoisie itself "furnishes the proletariat with weapons for fighting the bourgeoisie."[87] This has never been true. The bourgeoisie has made plenty of mistakes, but none of them big enough to provide a decisive weapon to the proletariat. The bourgeoisie's greatest weapons against itself are the self-interest, growth imperatives, and social impracticality of its own schemes. But where, exactly, is the bourgeoisie in the world today?

Entire sections of Marx's bourgeois class increasingly find themselves in the precarious class. What they have secured for themselves is precarious now, and those who can escape all forms of precarity are fewer and fewer. There is hardly anyone left in this world governed by capital who is not threatened by precarity. The exhaustion of capitalist logic in the world may very well not come from any battle or struggle, but from a world of humanity exhausted by life according to the logic capital.

In light of the complications of class analysis today, one of the key problems for Marx's hypothesis is that we cannot place our bets on a winning side. It is too hard to know what the sides are, never mind which one is winning. This undermines Marx's contention that there is clearly a revolutionary "class that holds the future in its hands."[88] This difficulty does not mean that revolution is impossible. It may even be inexorable and inevitable still. This only means that we have to accept the fact that revolution will not take the form of any grand stand-off between two hostile camps. People have been rethinking revolution ever since Marx theorized his particular version. Even contemporaneously with Marx, in the US, Henry David Thoreau's manifesto, *Civil Disobedience*, was published in 1849. There, he conceived

---

86   Scott, James C., *Domination and the Arts of Resistance: Hidden Transcripts* (Yale University Press, 1990).
87   Marx, op. cit., p. 19.
88   Ibid.

of something called "peaceable revolution."[89] For Thoreau, this did not mean a "legal revolution" (reform), but a revolution made by way of withdrawal as opposed to attack. Thoreau understood the necessity of a critical mass of withdrawal, and although he proposed breaking tax laws by refusal to pay, other forms of exodus, flight, and strike could be imagined and substituted. But instead of a long history of revolutionary reimagining, Edmund Burke and Karl Marx (following Thomas Hobbes and John Locke) have monopolized thinking on revolution such that it would reliably invoke the notion of "people" versus "sovereign" since the 17th century, a view still alive and well in the "Arab Spring" of 2011. Although Thoreau was not alone in a fairly long list of creative rethinkers of revolution from Marx to the present day, the conception of revolution from Hobbes and Locke has prevailed and has never been replaced. Fredric Jameson famously thought through the contention that we have a peculiar ability to imagine anything at all, except for the end of capitalism.[90] We are also impeded by the difficulty of imagining revolutionary alternatives to revolution.

Of all the precarious people standing face to face with one another today, none of them comprise a really revolutionary class. Pervasive global anxiety is the special and essential product of the present phase of capitalism.

The so-called lower middle class, the everyday worker, the artisan, in short, impoverished people everywhere, would of course like to abolish their own precarity. It is just not clear how to do so. Many within the precariat are not revolutionary, but conservative. Countless precarious people call upon capitalism to resolve the problems it gives rise to, seeking capitalist invention to address the crises of capitalism. So, the critique of capitalism is not necessarily developed from our precarity. Being revolutionary today depends, in part, upon a realization (or epiphany) that is not guaranteed by our precarity. A revolutionary sensibility is contingent upon the realization that growing precarity and global anxiety are features of capitalism.

The "dangerous class," the so-called social scum, have never been the "passively rotting mass" that Marx characterized them to be.[91] In some cases, as in the riots in France in 2005 and 2009, and those surrounding London in August of 2011, subsets of the population who

---

89   Thoreau, Henry David, *Civil Disobedience and Other Essays* (Dover, 1993), p.10.
90   Jameson, Fredric, "Future City," New Left Review 21, May-June 2003.
91   Marx, op. cit., p. 20.

are not part of anything recognizably "proletarian" make trouble for the mythological narratives of those societies. Earlier, throughout the 1990s, the Mexican Zapatistas showed that indigenous peoples who had never been integrated into the machinations of capitalist production, who were not "proletarian," could nonetheless throw the logic of capital into question. What is "social scum?" So-called social scum is the filthiest part of capitalism, a kind of residue that cannot be or has not yet been integrated into capitalist production, the human detritus that remains outside of the business cycles of exchange relations. From the unemployed or unemployable, to the unassimilated indigenous communities, the drug addicted and dropouts, institutionalized or freely wandering "psychotics," "neurotics," and other "patients," the homeless, and the whole underground circuitry of *sans-papiers* (the paperless, the unpermitted) everywhere, the so-called social scum remind us that capitalism is not a totality, for it cannot integrate everything into itself. There are always spheres of social life left out, forced out, living against or largely beyond the logic of capital. In this way, the "social scum" give us good news.

It is true that there is no such thing as a national economy, and that national economies have been disappearing since at least the late-18th century. Martha Nussbaum and Amartya Sen have demonstrated well that GDP and GNP measures of national wealth tell us little to nothing about who, within the internal populations of nations, actually has the money.[92] Following the critical research of Nussbaum and Sen, new measures have been developed and adopted at organizations such as the United Nations to try to better assess the real quality of life in nations, as opposed to GDP and GNP. We can now know with confidence that whenever political scientists and economists try to reassure us that national populations are doing better because of GNP growth, that they are either engaging in some form of manipulation or speaking out of ignorance. As cited above, even the neoliberal OECD is not so retrograde as to avoid publishing the truth about real and growing income inequality within the populations of its member nations. Capitalism must be a global system of exchange relations, its accumulation and growth imperatives require the supersession of national boundaries, and

---

92   See Nussbaum, Martha and Sen, Amartya, *The Quality of Life* (Oxford University Press, 1993), and Nussbaum, Martha, "Capabilities and Human Rights" in *Global Justice and Transnational Politics: Essays on the Moral and Political Challenges of Globalization* (The MIT Press, 2002).

no governor with any institutional influence wants to take responsibility for the affairs of capital. "Free trade" is the consensus of competing political parties in almost every country, already taken for granted in the liberal claptrap about "fair trade." In 1848, Marx claimed that "modern subjection to capital, the same in England as in France, in America as in Germany, has stripped him [the proletarian] of every trace of national character."[93] Taking America out of this list, Marx's vision of the supersession of nationality has in many ways been realized in Europeanization and the European Union, which have evolved following the lead of the business interests of capitalists in the European Coal and Steel Community and the European Economic Community during the deregulation craze of the 1980s and early 1990s. Nonetheless, patriotism still has powerful political uses, as can be seen during election cycles and wars, and a resilient "national character" of some parts of the precariat (the more conservative parts) can still make a comeback in periods of patriotic chauvinism. The ultimate fates of national identity and nationalism are still uncertain, and the resurgent resilience of patriotism remains an effective refuge of capitalist states.

Every class that gets the upper hand wants to keep the upper hand. "Becoming master" has been the most dangerous, overrated aspiration of politics, whether conventional or from below. Real autonomy in everyday life means that the logic of capital does not determine what one does and when one does it, and that human desire is never indefinitely postponed to the exhausted leftover hours after work, or worse, to retirement or fleeting holidays (if one even knows what to do with free time then). The achievement of real autonomy is not, however, possible through the individual activity of single persons alone, for it requires abolishing the present mode of appropriating and extracting our collective time and energies. When an individual person enjoys relatively high levels of autonomy in her everyday life, it might look to her as if real autonomy has been achieved or as if the relatively high level of autonomy that she enjoys is equally available to anyone. But politics depends upon the recognition of macrosocial realities, and we are incapable of politics for as long as we mistake our own experiences for everyone else's. The most transformative calling of the precariat is to destroy the actual causes, the macrosocial and macroeconomic conditions, of our growing and collective insecurity.

---

93 Marx, op. cit., p. 20.

Although the precarious people of the world are the immense majority, we can only speak in broad strokes about the shared interests of this immense majority. Although many precarious people have become accustomed to a functional high-anxiety, and although many might not know how to handle freedom from anxiety if they even had it, we can know one thing for certain: We made no conscious choice to give up our autonomy and health (both psychic and physical). Most of the world's precariat are integrated into what Franco Berardi has diagnosed as the frail psycho-sphere of the schizo-economy.[94] The ever diminishing populations of precarious people who are not using psychotropic drugs are nonetheless worrying about other aspects of survival and daily life. There is a form of anxiety for everyone today, to colonize human consciousnesses in a wide variety of ways. But present-day precarity is a peculiar impasse because it is a capitalist precarity that cannot be overcome through drugs, recreational sports, sex, vacations, retirement, and certainly not through policy, and thus, "the whole superincumbent strata of official society" must be "sprung into the air."[95]

Neither in substance, nor in form, is the struggle of the precariat a national struggle. Marx was as committed an internationalist as the world has ever known, already surpassing the commitments of fashionable forms of cosmopolitanism today. However, we still must finish cleaning out the cobwebs of the national thinking that obscured Marx's understanding of the logical order of revolution, that the "proletariat of each country must, of course, first of all settle matters with its own bourgeoisie."[96] Insurrectionary movements are not always national even if they have national locations and local agendas. As with the Zapatistas, some insurrectionary struggles are simultaneously subnational, national, distinctly local, and global all at once, in both form and substance. This could also be said about the "Arab Spring" and the Occupy movements of 2011, which were simultaneously about particular national *and* larger transnational issues. In *Unbounded Publics*, I called such movements "transgressive" to specify their violation of the national/transnational dichotomy.[97]

---

94 See Berardi, Franco "Bifo," *Precarious Rhapsody: Semiocapitalism and the Pathologies of the Post-alpha Generation* (Minor Compositions/Autonomedia, 2009), pp. 30-55.
95 Marx, op. cit., p. 20.
96 Ibid.
97 Gilman-Opalsky, Richard, *Unbounded Publics: Transgressive Public Spheres, Zapatismo, and Political Theory* (Lexington, 2008).

More importantly, as the trajectories of Lenin and Mao reveal, it is quite difficult, perhaps impossible, to move through the national context onto a transformative internationalism. The Russian and Chinese political movements of the 20th century never managed to shed their nationalisms, as many examples attest to, such as the Hungarian Uprising of 1956 where communists in Hungary demanded a non-Russian communism. National movements draw on nationalism to garner strength and mobilize support, and that nationalism cannot be shed so easily. The same concern could be found in Frantz Fanon's *The Wretched of the Earth*, where Fanon assures revolutionaries fighting against colonialism "that nationalism, that magnificent song that made the people rise against their oppressors, stops short, falters, and dies away on the day that independence is proclaimed."[98] Fanon warned against nationalism used for revolutionary purposes, that "if it is not enriched and deepened by a very rapid transformation into a consciousness of social and political needs, in other words into humanism, it leads up a blind alley."[99] Thus, Fanon held onto the Marxian theory of a withering nationalism as recently as 1961. Like Marx, Fanon expresses very clear reservations about nationalism and its dangers. But Marx's internationalism reflected his fear that communism would get stuck at the level of the nation-state, and the 20th century seems to have validated those fears. The internationalism of the "communism" of the 20th century was too much of an ideological gloss, backed up with government subsidies invested more for geopolitical strategizing than for the construction of a real global *Gemeinwesen*.

The question of violence cannot be answered in any categorical way. But, we cannot mean by violence the breaking of a law or the destruction of a car or a window, because even if breaking such things "harms" a person's finances, functioning as a pecuniary punishment, which in turn "harms" their ability to pay for things, the "violence" that comes from such breakings is too much the result of an indirect derivation, such that we can always make a further derivation and eventually find ourselves back to Pierre-Joseph Proudhon's declaration that property is itself theft, founded on some original robbery.[100] We have become accustomed to thinking of violence as a metaphor without noticing the abstraction. For example, too many people readily

---

98   Fanon, Frantz, *The Wretched of the Earth* (Grove Press, 1963), p. 203.
99   Ibid., p. 204.
100   Proudhon, Pierre-Joseph, *What is Property?* (Cambridge University Press, 1994).

speak of violence that results from accidents unrelated to the intentions of any person to do harm to any other person in particular. This is why we commonly say that an earthquake is violent, even though an earthquake means no harm to anything or anyone. Beyond the confusions of figurative speech mistaken as literal, it is also important to consider the capitalist rendering of violence, according to which absolute poverty is not violence, but occupying a public park without a permit may well be. Suffice it to say that the question of violence needs some unpacking. Nonetheless, we cannot say anything along the lines of Marx's claim that "the violent overthrow of the bourgeoisie lays the foundation for the sway of the proletariat."[101] When it comes to the precariat, what kind of violent overthrow do we have the will or the way to make? Much of the bourgeoisie has now moved inside the growing precarious class, and even if they are less precarious than others, their own hold on things is quite uncertain these days. The system of finance capital that has made the fortunes of the least precarious may very well be the system that will do them in.

Marxist historiography has held up quite well. Telling the stories of human societies through accounts of the antagonisms between haves and have-nots still helps do damage control on the pervasive influence of ideology on history. There are many ways to criticize and to improve upon Marx's approach, perhaps most importantly, to account for more antagonisms than only those that change relations on the world-historical scale. We can do a better Marxist history when we account for all the failed and fleeting oppositions to capitalist power. But alienation and estrangement have eclipsed the importance of oppression and exploitation. The latter still exist and examples abound. Yet, the question of the condition of our *species being*, or whatever concept is used to specify the existential subject, has been making a comeback. Human misery comes in many different flavors, and we do not really know if we want to be wealthy or well-educated or married or working in a big city with access to good restaurants. Everyone knows that there are droves of married people with college degrees in Manhattan who are also a miserable lot, who keep countless psychotherapists in booming business even while the rest of the economy breaks down. There is little (perhaps nothing) we can say with more certainty than that we want to be happy. But when it comes to specifying the content

101 Marx, op. cit., p. 21.

of that happiness we quickly encounter problems, for we scarcely know what happiness means for ones' own self. Life according to the logic of capital does not answer the question of happiness for us as we go, since there are so many other "more pressing" problems that we must address. Capitalism is simply unfit to guide us through life, unfit to rule on existential questions, unfit "to impose its conditions of existence upon society as an overriding law."[102] The logic of capital is incompetent of assuring us of an existence we desire. Society cannot forever rest on an operational logic that rationalizes and justifies our precarity in perpetuity.

The systematization of the pathological imperative to accumulate capital creates the essential conditions for the consolidation of human anxiety to the point of total insanity (the rationalization of every unreasonable thing), suicide, or collapse (whether from exhausting natural resources or from exhausting human nervous systems). Constant accumulation depends upon constant extraction and growth. Extraction and growth become more innovative, fracking methods are developed for natural gas while cellular technology is "fracking" cognitive resources from workers everywhere. The least precarious among us have been betting for some time on their own survival as a matter of chance or of luck, or in the hopes for one or another surprising fix by legislators, scientists, or industry (which includes the military). Post-Fordist, post-industrial capitalism cuts out from under its feet the very foundation on which it stands – by making people everywhere more and more precarious, by making the system of accumulation more and more precarious, the anxiety of the precariat is also the anxiety of the system. Capitalism tests not only the limits of accumulation, but also, the "stress limit" of the whole society. Today, even the gravediggers are anxious, as their average annual pay stagnates at just under $30,000 (as of 2011) while the cost of living keeps on rising. No outcome is inevitable, but we do have imaginations, and some outcomes are preferable to others.

---

102 Ibid.

II.

Precarious Communists and "Communism"

"You will never need to worry about a steady income."[103]

IN WHAT RELATION DO PRECARIOUS COMMUNISTS STAND TO "COMMU-nism"?

Precarious communists are never hopeful about any political party on Earth, even, if not especially, self-named "communist" or other working-class parties from the 20th century or today. This includes Syriza, a party that "communists" like Slavoj Žižek (not a precarious communist) expressed far too much optimism about recently.[104]

The precariat includes most of us, and therefore has diverse interests, is internally pluralistic, and often self-contradictory. Beyond the general features of its precarity, there is little (if not nothing) that we can specify about it. In this way, it is less a socio-economic class and more a massive group of groups. There is also little that is unitary about the smaller group of groups called precarious communists, which is why they cannot settle upon a detailed cohesive platform, but can only express general directions punctuated with specific goals as nodal points in the development of particular movements.

---

103 Fortune cookie, Springfield, IL, Monday, July 23, 2012.
104 Slavoj Žižek delivered a speech on Sunday, June 3, 2012 entitled "The heart of the people of Europe beats in Greece" which was hosted by Syriza.

Precarious communists comprise just some part, and some relatively small part, of the global precariat. The majority of the precariat is not communist. Precarious communists have neither the confidence nor the influence to set up sectarian principles that would shape and mold their movements. This does not mean their movements are defeatist or accidental, but rather, experimental and self-conscious.

Precarious communists are distinguished from "communists" in the following ways: 1. They point out and bring to the front that capitalism, an ideology and system of life driven by the accumulation of capital, and the cultural-valuational norms and material reality of existing capitalist society – *in short, that capital itself* – is at the root of the most pressing problems of all forms of precarity. Unlike "communists," precarious communists are also precarious about communism itself. Precarious communists prefer and defend the internal logic of communism, the notion of the overall health of the commons, and they prefer and defend the cultural-valuational norms of communism, which centrally include an ethical obligation to others (i.e., *Sittlichkeit*). They prefer and defend other possible material realities than those of capitalism, realities that they can variously imagine and represent. But precarious communists distrust all political parties, nationally framed struggles, and conventional or institutional remedies, even if they do favor some over others. 2. In the various stages of development which the multiple movements of the precariat must pass through, they always and everywhere assess the relation of the problem to capital, and work precariously toward an experimental and self-conscious communism.

Precarious communists, therefore, are equipped with sharp anarchist sensibilities, and/or have a good understanding of the history of revolutionary movements. Large subsets of the precariat are not precarious communists inasmuch as they seek to address their own precarity through political parties, legislation, capitalist and technological innovations, by accident or by luck, by an even more unhinged "free market," or by the statist delusions of past "communists." In this way, precarious communists are the only ones who maintain a political consciousness of the limitations of all of the above, and thus, theoretically, they have the advantage of a practical understanding of the conditions and possibilities for changing the world.

There is no one immediate aim of precarious communists, and nowhere is the conquest of political power their aim. But everywhere, and in any creative manner, precarious communists critically observe, represent, and try to exacerbate the breaking apart of both the ideological and material bases of existing society and its operational logic.

The theoretical positions of precarious communists are in no way based on ideas or principles that have been invented, or discovered, by some professional philosopher, for philosophy is often done better by events. Sometimes, a riot or revolt is a work of philosophy inasmuch as it raises penetrating questions about the world in which it occurs. Good philosophy has always thrown the world as we knew it into question. Sometimes, social movements accomplish that defining goal better than books. We do not know, or necessarily care, what precarious communists are reading, for we know that they are already philosophical. Ideology is far too certain for anxious, precarious people; uncertainty is the enemy of ideology. Uncertainty has been the oxygen of philosophy, going all the way back to Socrates. Uncertainty gives philosophy what it needs to breathe. To be precarious is to have more questions than answers, and to be unsettled by uncertainty is the very disposition of philosophy. Precarious communists need not see themselves as philosophers in their ongoing, searching, uncertainty, for they are living philosophy directly. Precarity is the origin of and impetus for all good philosophy. Unwavering sureness is the pretension of ideology, the pretension of a self-assured worldview that settles every question in its own favor. Unwavering sureness is the opposite of a philosophical disposition.

Unlike other precarious people, precarious communists try to consciously confront and give expression to the problems of capital. The Zapatistas and many of their supporters, the anticapitalist globalization protestors of 1999 (Seattle) and 2001 (Genoa), many who participated in the "Arab Spring", and many in the Occupy movements, are precarious communists. To be sure, they are not "communists" in any old sense, but they engage in a precarious communism. Indeed, the movements of precarious communism may go by many names, but they are often going on right before our eyes.

Precarious communists understand that property relations remain a problem, as the recent trope of "the 99%" versus "the 1%" clearly expresses. The slogan points out growing and objectionable disparities in the ownership of wealth and property, and thus, in security. The growth of such disparities, i.e., in income and security levels, does not need to be maintained, even may be impossible to maintain, and yet capitalism is forthrightly on the side of its continuation.

The French Revolution aimed, in part, to abolish feudal property, but it was nonetheless not a revolution against capitalism, nor could it have been. Revolutions sometimes happen within the limits of capital and for other reasons, but inasmuch as the logic of capital survives them, we move on with another unacceptable state of affairs, with new forms of precarity. We cannot be so brazen as to deny real qualitative improvements between two states of affairs. But if, for example, the Egyptian Revolution of 2011 takes place entirely within the limits of capital, then the Egyptians will have the Muslim Brotherhood to betray them next, instead of Hosni Mubarak, and after a while, a new precarity will compel the people to return to Tahrir Square. That is exactly what has happened. We witnessed the awe-inspiring reclamation of Tahrir Square in revolt against the new president, Mohamed Morsi, in November 2012.

The distinguishing feature of precarious communism is not the abolition of either precarity or of capitalism totally, but rather, the destruction of capitalist mythologies, what I have previously called "spectacular capitalism."[105] It is critical to emphasize that spectacular capitalism does not only function on an ideological terrain, for it is materialized in the real choices and organization of everyday life everywhere, shaping everything from wages and market regulations to urban planning and development and the prevailing visual environment of cities and towns. Actually existing capitalism hides behind the mythology of spectacular capitalism, making it difficult to see the causal relationships between capital and our precarity, and thus, capitalist mythology is the last defense of the system of constant accumulation. The more the logic of capital is exposed as causally related to the central problems of human life, the more precarious people become precarious communists. The art of "exposé" is, therefore, central to the politics of precarious communism.

The theory of precarious communists cannot be summed up in any single sentence, which is good news for us and bad news for those who would slander the movements of the precariat.

Nonetheless, precarious communists have been reproached as "communists," as ones who conspire with liberals to steer the apparatus of big government to tax the rich out of existence and to regulate

---

105 See *Spectacular Capitalism* (Minor Compositions/Autonomedia, 2011). The mythology of spectacular capitalism is first defined and discussed in the "Introduction: *A Priori*" of that book.

everything, or even more absurdly, as ones who celebrate the achievements and visions of Mao or of Stalin. Precarious communists are reproached through such deliberate mischaracterizations (a) because precarious communists are not in the world by way of a class, party, or movement with a shared name or cohesive agenda, and are beyond reproach as such and (b) because "communism" is not beyond reproach as one of the decisive villains of the 20ᵗʰ century. The historically effective strategy of capitalists blaming every failure on "communism" has been making a comeback. Reproaches come from the precarity of the least precarious among us, for example from "the 1%" and their circle of defenders, because the peculiar anxiety of the least precarious is that they have a lot to lose (and they want to keep it that way).

Marx understood well that a key feature of the capitalist mythology was to say that whoever has much wealth (i.e., stored up capital) and property (i.e., land, commodities, luxuries) has acquired these things through their own hard work, and that if you want wealth and property, hard work will get them for you. Today, this mythology is still asserted everywhere by the defenders of capital. This problem stems back before Marx, at least to John Locke, who argued in his Chapter "Of Property," that (1) one has a rightful claim of ownership over whatever he produces by his own labor, that (2) he has an obligation to not take more than could be used before spoiling, but that (3) in terms of things like diamonds, gold, or silver, things not "really useful to the life of man," one could store up as much of those "durable" things as he likes because they only have a value set by "fancy or agreement," and no real use.[106] What Locke did not foresee was that (1) capitalism would sever ownership from labor through the wage system, which would make both the workers and their work the private property of other people, that (2) the accumulation and growth imperatives of capitalism would be incompatible with his recommended limits on the extraction of natural resources, and that (3) diamonds, gold, and silver would be given use-values (not merely exchange-values) the more that they became replacements for labor to the point that whoever has money can purchase the things necessary and useful to life, independently of their own work. Marx might have been more of a liberal if the capitalists actually followed Locke's recommendations in *Two Treatises of Government: The Second Treatise of Civil Government*.

---

106 Locke, op. cit., Chapter 5, "Of Property," Section 46, p. 342.

The problem is that capitalism cannot abide the laws or aspirations of classical liberalism because it is capitalism. Defenders of capitalism today know well that the three Lockean premises above cannot be abided. Those who would seek to subject capital today to Locke's rules on our natural rights to private property would immediately be defamed as "socialists."

Who has property and wealth, and of what form, still matters, but Marx placed too much emphasis on bourgeois private property. Marx held that this form of property was the irreducible core of capitalist society, and that abolishing it would strike at the heart of the capitalist system.

But hasn't capitalism shown an amazing ability to rethink and redefine public and private, even to make the private into the public and the public into the private, and to survive and to thrive on such innovation?

Public parks are treated like private property, yet to get permission to use them, especially for a protest demonstration, the actual public must negotiate with public institutions, which manage them like private firms letting land for weddings and birthday parties. When publics make political use of public parks, cities call in reinforcements from the police. In what meaningful ways do public parks belong to the public? Does anyone still believe the lie that public education is a real public property? Public universities were privatized in the US in the 1980s, and European austerity has been accelerating that phase at an alarming rate. What passes for public health care in the US is run by private for-profit corporations. Public libraries are closed without mutiny or murmur because they have been emptied of the public itself. To maintain public space, the public now needs to occupy it defiantly. Where are the new public spaces? You can find new public spaces in privately owned cafes, and perhaps most oddly, in Barnes & Noble bookstores. Barnes & Noble invites the public inside to sit on its floors and read books, to freely congregate, to enjoy the free air conditioning and Wi-Fi, and not to purchase anything at all. Capitalism has converted loitering into a commendable act of public association with capitalist aspirations. But Barnes & Noble may not exist much longer. They are closing more locations than they're opening, largely because bookstores can't compete with the internet, the latest privatized public space – a contradiction in terms, human association without human association. And when the Barnes & Noble stores close down, we will lament the loss of that privately owned public space, whereas not long before, Barnes & Noble was the villain who was everywhere shutting down the locally owned bookshops. In recent movements, it has become a joke that most of the poor and unemployed participants in the "Arab Spring" and Occupy Wall Street were glued to their smartphones, subscribing to services that charge activists a portion of the discretionary income they claim they don't have. There is, of course, some truth in this bad joke. Those who occupy the subject position of the old proletariat have been allowed to play with the toys of the bourgeoisie.

So, instead of the old fixation on bourgeois private property, we should be focusing on anxiety, precarity, and importantly, on acceleration. Paul Virilio's work on dromology (from the ancient Greek, *dromos*, meaning race course) focuses on the logic of speed and is critical to our understanding of the role of acceleration in capitalism today.[107] Virilio contends: "Our societies have become arrhythmic. Or they only know one rhythm: constant acceleration. Until the crash and systemic failure... We lack a political economy of speed... we will need one... A world of immediacy and simultaneity would be absolutely uninhabitable."[108] Capital has always demanded constant accumulation, but increasingly, it also demands constant acceleration. This dimension of speed is critical to understanding our anxiety. "Yes, speed causes anxiety by the abolition of space or more precisely by the failure of collective thinking on real space because relativity was never truly understood or secularized."[109] Instantaneity means that we have to move without reflection, that we have to act decisively without the safeguards of careful thought. Capital can transform itself in new directions without undermining its own logic, so its latest demands for high-speed do not replace its historical dependency on accumulation. But always, capitalism has to balance its evolving aspirations with new efforts to suppress our collective anxiety and to avert radical criticism.

To be a capitalist is to take certain positions, which can be acted on with others, either consciously in line with, or directly in defense of, the logic of capital. What does this mean? Fundamentally, a capitalist

---

107 Paul Virilio, one of the most important theorists for those interested in precarity, has written extensively on the relationship of speed to anxiety. Although any number of his books could be recommended, I would suggest *Speed and Politics: An Essay on Dromology* (Semiotext(e), 2006) and *The Administration of Fear* (Semiotext(e), 2012).

108 Virilio, Paul, *The Administration of Fear* (Semiotext(e), 2012), pp. 27 and 37.

109 Ibid., p. 32.

will not see the dictatorship of capital as problematic, or worse, cannot see the dictatorship of capital at all. To the capitalist, a dictator is only ever a man, whereas capitalism is the worldview of all those opposed to dictatorships today. So, the capitalist wants to strengthen capitalism, even to save it from itself in periods of its own peril. Despite this, few capitalists have escaped the pervasive anxiety of unending accumulation and acceleration, and many capitalists are precarious. We must therefore acknowledge that just as there are precarious communists there are also precarious capitalists. The precariat is not full of people with equal levels of precarity, some are more precarious than others, and the precariat is ideologically and philosophically heterogeneous. Precarious capitalists understand the volatility and uncertainty of capitalism as a system, they understand its problems, and they live with the insecurity of that knowledge and reality. Hence, precarity does not guarantee a communist sensibility. But then again, socio-economic class position does not guarantee a communist sensibility either.

Capital is a limited power with unlimited aspirations that slowly disclose its limitations.

When, therefore, capital is channelled into new projects designed for continued or accelerated accumulation and for the further consolidation of the wealth and property of its beneficiaries, even then, it does not solve the problems of its own precarity.[110]

Let us now consider wages and salaries as possible antidotes to precarity.

Wages and salaries incentivize work, variously enable our material subsistence, and compel people everywhere to reproduce capitalism through everyday life. It is therefore completely impractical to simply denounce wages and salaries as an objectionable feature of capitalism, for some movements against capital may demand higher wages and higher salaries. Capitalism always aims to minimize expenditure and maximize profit (accumulation depends on this formula), and profit margins are maximized in part by keeping wages and salaries (expenditure) far lower than incomes and revenues. A practical member of the precariat must, even if it is not her only initiative, pursue more wages and salary, while the logic of capital simultaneously requires

---

110 From a dromological perspective, there is no escape velocity from precarity. This is, again, related to Virilio's research on the relationship between high-speed and high anxiety.

resisting such added costs. The central problem of this practical conflict of interest is that the precarious person often misidentifies the
cause of her precarity in insufficient wages or salaries.

Even though job security is rarely related to wages and salary, the
worker often accepts the misperception that higher pay will solve the
problems of precarity. Since the life and times of Marx, working people everywhere have sought to reconcile their precarity with the help
of unions, labor laws, and other favorable legislation involving things
like health benefits and ombudsmen. Marx understood the appeal of
this pathway, and while he encouraged the improvement of working
conditions, he was rightly suspicious of the premises underlying such
initiatives. If we can always negotiate a better deal with our bosses,
then our work (and our bosses) will become more tolerable, and if our
work is more tolerable, then we will become less antagonistic. Why
risk the danger of making revolution if one can safely accomplish one's
goals through contractual negotiations within the limits of the existing system? There are two major problems here, only one of which
Marx observed. First, Marx understood that the worker "is allowed
to live only in so far as the interest of the ruling class requires it."[111]
So, even if conditions are tolerable, the worker has no real autonomy
from the demands of capital. Working life is made more tolerable only
in so far as the interests of the employing class are not jeopardized by
such provisions. Second, we have discovered that no amount of wages
or salaries can eliminate the reasonable anxiety of precarious people,
and that wages can go up alongside growing insecurities in the system
of accumulation. More money does not, therefore, mean less anxiety.
Growing anxiety and precarity are permanent features of the system.

In our societies, most (not all) work is a means to accumulate
capital, and everyone knows it. Even if not directly, our work is ultimately subjected to some market logic. If we are doing unpaid work
on things that we are not selling, for example, certain forms of artist,
activist, volunteer, or service work, we inevitably end up doing such
work after some other form of work we call a job. Precarious communists distinguish themselves from precarious capitalists in many
ways, but foremost in that we do not happily accept work as a means
to life. A full-time life of everyday work colonizes a person's entire
wakeful state, even for the unemployed, who are colonized by the

---

111 Marx, op. cit., p. 24.

material needs associated with *not* working. Precarious communists have a communist disdain for this situation and imagine a joyful and autonomous work, motivated (at least in part) by an interest in the radical transformation of the conditions and quality of everyday life.

Inasmuch as we have direct experiences with joyful and autonomous work today, they mostly take place in our leftover "spare time." But leftover "spare time" is increasingly rare, in many cases non-existent until retirement, and retirement is all the time more postponed by, for example, laws in the spirit of austerity. While precarious communists have a communist disdain for this, they do not have any confident solutions. Precarious communists are communists without certainty, without any enduring political confidence, but this does not mean that they don't know much. Their uncertainty about politics is itself a condition and reflection of knowledge. A precarious communist also knows in her most meaningful lived experiences – perhaps in love, in tragedy, in playing with a young child, in the creative moments of art or recreation, in the euphoria of musical bliss, in the awe of visual vistas, and of human intimacy – that the logic of capital is absent there, for such experiences have a different *logos* altogether.

Any express interest in abolishing the capitalist organization of anything is wrongly viewed, from the point of view of capital, as "communist," as some dangerous desire for huge government bureaucracy, as the abolition of individuality and freedom! But there is nothing in the precarious communism of today that embodies a desire for government bureaucracies. Moreover, individuality and freedom are far more constrained – in some cases abolished – when everything a person does, or can do, is subordinated to the logic of capital.

The word and concept freedom have been degraded by capitalist distortion, and Marx understood this well when he wrote that, under capitalism, freedom means nothing more than "free trade, free selling and buying."[112] Today, this mutilated meaning remains central to the mythology of spectacular capitalism. For example, consider the right-wing author Mark Levin who uncritically repeats the abuses that (1) all opposition to the free market must invariably come from the villain known as "the Statist" and that (2) freedom essentially refers to the freedom of businessmen to engage in capitalist exchange relations.[113]

---

112 Ibid., p. 25.
113 See Levin, Mark, *Liberty and Tyranny: A Conservative Manifesto* (Simon & Schuster, 2009), especially Chapter 6 "On the Free Market."

Levin saw emergences like Occupy Wall Street as part of the Obama campaign, and thus scarcely understood the disaffection expressed there. For ideological reasons, Levin cannot recognize, and is perhaps incapable of understanding, the long history of anti-statist communism that was contemporaneous with Marx and developed throughout the 20th century, let alone Marx's own complex theory of the state. Levin's defense of his own deranged notion of freedom can be found at the heart of capitalist mythology today, but it never escapes or refutes Marx's old criticism: Freedom defined as the freedom to engage in capitalist exchange relations (or, more simply, the freedom of capital) is not freedom at all. In fact, freedom is exactly the opposite of Levin's narrow conception. A real, substantive sense of human freedom would have to be defined by what we can do in the space and time *beyond* capitalist exchange relations. For example, we are much closer to the truth when we calculate our "free time" as the sum total of time that we are *not* working. This is partly acknowledged already in the common contention that we are "free" on the weekends, or that we are "not free" until after work.

We cannot continue to allow capitalism to make freedom mean nothing more than the freedom of capital. If freedom depends upon – or is defined by – the "freedom" of free market capitalism, then "capital" becomes a precondition for freedom. As long as freedom is defined by capital, the two terms, freedom and capital, are made mutually dependent on one another.[114]

"Communism" still horrifies capitalists, because the acceleration of the capitalist form of freedom (i.e., the widespread deregulation of the private sector globally throughout the 1980s and 1990s) largely coincided with the movement against and the collapse of 20th century "communism." Capitalists like Levin still express abject horror at the thought of any countervailing force to capitalism, even though the presence of real threats to the dictatorship of capital are few and far between. Capitalist horror thus takes the form of anxiety.[115] The least

---

114 This very relationship, of the codependency of capital and freedom, is what Milton Friedman argued in defense of, long before Mark Levin, in *Capitalism and Freedom* (The University of Chicago Press, 1962).

115 At this juncture, in the correlated paragraphs of the 1848 manifesto, Marx begins writing "you" to address his adversaries, as in, "You are horrified..." and begins writing "we" to refer to the communists. I follow these turns as I see fit. First of all, unlike Marx, I have no confidence that my text will be read by my adversaries. That would be nice, but can by no means be counted on. Second,

precarious capitalists want total freedom, defined in their narrow way, and they want legal reassurances that would effectively ameliorate their minor anxieties. But in their society, the comfort of confidence and any *real* freedom (besides that of consumer choice) "is already done away with for nine-tenths of the population; its existence for the few is solely due to its non-existence in the hands of those nine-tenths."[116]

In the famous quote above, Marx is talking about an issue of disparity that has recently been given new and widespread circulation. The Occupy movements of 2011 and 2012 intensified Marx's "nine-tenths," moving to sharper invocations of "the 99%." Macroeconomic data attests to this more radical thesis, and it is true that even Marx did not imagine the disparities that exist today in terms of property and wealth. But much of the Marxian sentiment resonates still: Precarious communists want to do away with the ascendency of the capitalist form of freedom, the necessary condition for whose existence is the global subordination of real human freedoms to the interests of capital.

Precarious communists would like to do away with a system that generates growing anxiety and precarity indefinitely. Precarious communists understand that growing anxiety and precarity are inevitable features of the indefinite accumulation and acceleration of capital. As communists, we would destroy capitalism, but as precarious communists, we don't know how.

From the moment that there is any imposition on the freedom of businessmen to do as they wish, from the moment that resistances from below destabilize their self-serving social order, capital's loyal spokesmen speak of the end of freedom, the beginning of terrorism, the irrationality of riots, and always once again, the threat of "communism."

By "freedom," our opponents mean their own particular freedoms, the freedoms of the least precarious among us, and the potential freedoms of hopeful precarious capitalists. The precarious capitalist is not entirely decided *for* capital, and he could be brought to the point of an ultimate precarity, to the point at which maintaining a capitalist worldview would become indefensible, and personally, impractical.

Precarious communism deprives no one of anything, except that it strives to deprive capitalist mythology of its historic power to

---

"we communists" are a fragmentary and heterogeneous assemblage, often dissipated, so the consistent use of the inclusive pronoun is problematic here.

116 Marx, op. cit., p. 25.

effectively rationalize all forms of unfairness (including exploitation) and alienation (including our own unhappiness).

It is often objected that without a world organized by the logic of capital, all innovation will cease, and laziness will replace energetic hard work.

According to this, energetic hard work is what people bring to the capitalist workplace every morning! The history of human innovation and hard work is typically imagined to have really begun with the mode of mass production associated with industrialization, for preindustrial subsistence production is far less ambitious. Anecdotally, students in my classes on Marx commonly express an inability to imagine human survival without a mode of production that is really quite new, that dates only back the 18th century. It is easy to correct the problem because no one can gainsay that human history stretches back to far before industrialization. This does not mean we should long for the 17th century. It means we must think more critically about incentives, innovation, and laziness. Is anyone convinced that, without capital, people would never make experiments, would never explore new forms of art and communication, and only make love with dreadful laziness, because all of their passionate motivations derive from an interest in getting paid? Also, hasn't the history of crime shown us that innovation often flourishes in the absence of capital, in the context of poverty? Plato understood this point well in *The Republic*, where Socrates claims that both luxury and poverty lead to the danger of innovation.[117] But in the view from capital, "innovation" is given an uncritical normative endorsement, which assumes that all new (especially technological) developments are always good for the world. This position holds that, without the logic of capital to motivate and incentivize us, we would laze around or languish in a society that none could bear. One of the peculiarities of this normative position is that it portrays the most unbearable uncertainties of our present precarity, as not only perfectly bearable, but also, as clearly preferable to any alternative.

All objections levelled against communism in the early years of the millennium are in fact objections to "communism." These objections are often expressions of a precarious capitalism that is worried about its own future.

---

117 *The Republic of Plato: Second Edition* (Basic Books, 1991), Book IV, *422a*, p. 99.

Marx's materialism ensured that he wrote sparingly (though, not nothing) about capitalist culture. He held that capitalist culture was "for the enormous majority, a mere training to act as a machine."[118] Culture consists of the whole discursive terrain on which valuational norms, social mores, and ethical obligations are inculcated, and on which ideology functions, including the intergenerational transmission of religious worldviews, national, sub-national, or ethnic self-understandings. Culture is the cumulative and collective product of education by every means, formal and informal, good and bad. Culture provides the context of our relationality. Culture often obscures reality, because it is comprised of perspectives that accommodate the world as it is, that are not merely *from* but actively *for* this world. This was Marx's concern, so he tried to cut through culture in order to get directly to reality itself, developing a method for the task. But capitalist culture also effectively shapes reality, making the world of facts what it is. This point was better understood by 20th century philosophers, through the help of psychoanalysis, and from Georg Lukács to German and French critical theory.

Marx viewed culture as a superstructural phenomenon. He accused his adversaries thusly: "Your very ideas are but the outgrowth of the conditions of your bourgeois production and bourgeois property, just as your jurisprudence is but the will of your class made into a law for all, a will whose essential character and direction are determined by the economic conditions of existence of your class."[119] Marx was wrong to place structure and superstructure in a unidirectional causal relationship, and this is old news. As many others have pointed out, including Gramsci, Lukács, Adorno, Horkheimer, and Debord, the real dialectic travels in both directions, often at the same time. Inasmuch as economic conditions are manmade, they are made by the conscious activities, policies, and other decisions of wilful human actors who are not simply motivated by the material conditions of life. Ideology always plays a role. Gramsci explained this in 1917 in his short essay on the ideological causes of the Russian Revolution, "The Revolution Against *Capital*." "The Bolshevik Revolution consists more of ideologies than of events."[120] What Gramsci was highlighting

---

118 Marx, op. cit., p. 26.
119 Ibid.
120 Gramsci, Antonio, "The Revolution Against *Capital*" in *The Antonio Gramsci Reader: Selected Writings 1916 – 1935* (New York University Press, 2000), p. 33.

in this essay was that historical materialism could be derailed, sped up, or impeded by ideological impetuses, and that ideology could really change human relations and things in the world, as was happening in Russia. This was one of the reasons why, shortly after Marx's death, the next generation of Marxists could not maintain the view of culture as merely superstructural, as affect without effect.

The idea that capitalism is nothing more than the inevitable outcome of the laws of nature, that capitalism is an expression of human nature itself, is a persistent misconception that should have been eradicated by sociology a long time ago. Humans always act in social contexts; *how we act* mostly reflects the nature of one social context or another, and not the nature of humanity as such. Some sociologists, including Marx, are suspicious of human nature to the point of questioning its existence – all we have are humans and their conditions of life. Today, human nature has made a comeback by way of neuropsychology and cognitive science. For example, we can speak of what the body (or specifically, the brain) can do – how it does what is does – as a concrete human nature, as a substance that can only work in particular ways, which we can now understand empirically. We can speak of differently natured children and infants with renewed reassurance, that is, not only with sociology, but with biology too. Yet, what the body does in fact – *what we are doing in the world* – is always done within some social context or another. Much (even if not all) of the intersubjective, interpersonal, and perceived meaning of what a body does, of what bodies (and brains) are busy doing, belongs to the category of culture. Admittedly, culture cannot answer every question. Neither can ideology. Neither can the materialist discourses of natural and social science.

A family is, among other things, a small economy, complete with internal divisions of labor and its own distinctive culture. The family is, in part, a necessary microcosm of the society at large. Its smaller size allows us to see that the logic of capital is not totalitarian there. To be sure, the family is a capitalist sphere, as its internal affairs are inevitably subjected to the capital at its disposal, how it utilizes its capital in the related markets, for example, in housing, utilities, food, entertainment, security, insurance, education, and mobility. The affairs of the family are governed by capital, but never entirely.

In error, Marx wrote about "the bourgeois family" as a unitary form. There is perhaps nothing unitary about any class of family, except that families tend to be the location of both the healthiest and the sickest social contexts in a person's life. The family puts its members through some of the most traumatic lessons, many that are impossible to overcome in a lifetime. At the same time, most families offer something better than trauma, a place of some belonging, and in the best case, of permanent love and reliable affection. Thus, a family could be a peculiar kind of property, one that is not contingent upon capital – something that one has without having money. Marx oversimplifies the family unit as an arrangement based "on capital, on private gain."[121] As mentioned, this is part of the story, but the family is more complex and paradoxical. The family is often the last refuge of the unemployed, the downsized, the imprisoned, or of those with severe disabilities. At the same time, much like in society, the family can turn against its own members, if a young adult openly claims a "despised" sexuality or breaks too many of the house rules, or in cases of abuse. There are countless variations. The family imbricates its individual members with an intimate exposure to capitalist exchange relations in miniature, but also, to the importance of a communist logic, where certain comforts and commitments are guaranteed by the ethical dimensions of *Gemeinwesen*, not by an interest in accumulation or acceleration.

The problems of family life cannot be solely attributed to its being as capitalism-in-miniature. It is unlikely that the end of capitalism would rid the family of its traumatic tendencies. Young children, in particular, are subjected to some of the worst nightmares by their parents, and capital cannot be blamed for all that private terror.

Jürgen Habermas has diagnosed other problems of what he called "familial-vocational privatism," which refers to a narrow fixation on home life and careerism, acculturated by capitalism.[122] Habermas describes how the bourgeois acculturations of family life have centralized an "achievement ideology" and various forms of privatism that make it a virtue to turn inward and limit concern to one's own small sphere of affection.[123] This stems from the emphasis on individuation and privatization in the logic of capital. The family is a small community, with some actively communist dimensions, but it is also a highly privatized space that removes and protects us from the wider world of human association, thus making only a small private allowance for communist

---

121 Marx, op. cit., p. 26.
122 See Habermas, Jürgen, *Legitimation Crisis* (Beacon Press, 1975), pp. 75-79.
123 Ibid., p. 81.

human relations: "Some communism for us," the family seems to say, internally and defensively, but not with others elsewhere. On any given suburban street, in any given residential neighborhood, there is a good deal of communism within each family unit, but scarcely any between them. Especially in times of crisis, the bunker mentality of familial-vocational privatism reveals itself, as every family home becomes a panic room.

Capitalist education! In existing society, there is a certain disservice in teaching young people about human solidarity, ethical obligations to others, and the necessity of interdependency. In present conditions of culture and economy, a student who goes from school into the existing society is far better equipped if she has learned to count on no one else, to be self-interested, and to fully secure one's own well-being before getting side-tracked by voluntary aid to others. Thus, familial-vocational privatism and the achievement ideology are inculcated from a young age through the educational system. In many liberal arts colleges throughout the US, there has been a counter-movement trying to build into general education curricula such things as "engaged citizenship," "the virtues of service," "global awareness," "social responsibility," and other noble orientations. These are just the old virtues of "public education," and they have only become a counter-movement in light of growing privatization. The problem is that such schools, though committed to a good idea of citizenship, do not adequately recognize the incompatibility of their liberal mission with the capitalist world surrounding them.

But the logic of capital does not simply surround the university, for it reorganizes the university from inside. Increasingly, education is governed by the marketability of its courses and degree programs, and especially, by assessments of what those degrees can guarantee for graduates moving out into the capitalist lifeworld. David Horowitz has argued that universities are more and more overrun by communist revolutionaries who want to destroy capitalism, despite the fact that such imaginary institutions could not even survive in the existing world.[124] Tuition has been replacing publicly subsidized education in the US since at least 1967 when then-Governor Ronald Reagan argued that public education was too expensive and that California's

---

124 Horowitz, David and Laskin, Jacob, *One-Party Classroom: How Radical Professors at America's Top Colleges Indoctrinate Students and Undermine Our Democracy* (Random House, 2009).

universities should be privatized and shifted onto a tuition basis.[125] In the 1980s, now as president, Reagan successfully worked to introduce tuition at public universities throughout the country. Today, throughout Europe, the privatization of public education is on the austerity fast track.

Parents have begun to raise behavioral questions about young children who can't sit still for an hour to watch a television show. Parents may be alarmed if their children can't navigate an iPad or send a text message by the age of 5 or 6 years old. They may have them tested for ADD or ADHD. The current parent-generation can hardly consider the possibility that their own distractions are a bore to the unruly interests of a child. So a new anxiety emerges, which is a complete reversal of the old one. Once, a parent would worry about too much TV (in the 1970s) and too much video games (in the 1980s), whereas today the concern is turned upside down, and is about not enough TV and not enough video games. The new parental anxiety is about the child's too-slow integration into the accelerated world of cellular technology and all of its accoutrements. Precarious communists do not express nostalgia for the way that things were in the 1950s or in the 1990s, but that doesn't prevent us from making critical diagnoses of the latest maladies.

Let us consider the relationship of precarious communism to feminism.

The precarious communist favors the more radical trajectories of feminism, preferring those of Valerie Solanas, Silvia Federici, Nancy Fraser, Judith Butler, Sheila Rowbotham, or bell hooks over thinkers like Betty Friedan, Susan Brownmiller, Naomi Wolf, or Susan Moller Okin. The latter group define the goals of feminism as achievable within the limits of capitalist society. Within communist theorization, one always looks for the critique of and the relation to capital and its logic. Many radical feminists today are interested in what could be called "gender precarity," which expresses an anxiety about gender and its historical, supposed certainty, and about our ability to perform at the level of gendered expectations. Judith Butler's *Gender Trouble* and Michael Warner's *The Trouble with Normal*, for example, are centrally concerned with the precarity of gender.[126] Feminists and

---

125 "Universities: Tuition or Higher Taxes," Time Magazine, Friday, Feb. 17, 1967.

126 Butler, Judith, *Gender Trouble: Feminism and the Subversion of Identity* (Routledge, 1990); Warner, Michael, *The Trouble with Normal: Sex, Politics, and the*

feminism have always been precarious from a political point of view, that is, always narrowly averting forms of cooptation on the one hand, and premature claims of a "post-feminist" irrelevance on the other. Feminism reveals that precarity is not simply a villain, not something only worthy of denunciation. Gender precarity, for example, makes possible new forms of becoming. This can be seen not only in Butler's feminism, but also, in Nancy Fraser's call for gender deconstruction, Drucilla Cornell's call for transformations, and Félix Guattari's call for becoming-woman.[127] The uncertainty of precarity, from within the radical feminist imaginary, creates a space for productive subversions, in which we can create and recreate ourselves. "Third-wave" feminism and queer theory, because they are especially focused on the precariousness of gender, are especially useful in this regard. But also, Silvia Federici's feminist and autonomist Marxist attention to the everyday lives and unpaid labor of women, highlights other dimensions of precarity.[128]

In light of this, and on the whole, feminism deepens and enriches the theory of precarity and the position of precarious communism and should be autonomously integrated into the critical dispositions of precarious communists everywhere, inasmuch as such integration makes sense.

With the exception of certain apologists, everyone knows that sexism and heterosexism persist. Capital continues its consolidation on the grounds of sexist and heterosexist worldviews and practices. Women continue to cost less than men because equal pay for equal work is only true *de jure*, not *de facto*, and so much of "women's work" is not even paid for at all. The cultural mainstream in every country still assumes heterosexuality as the normative basis of plots and fictive narratives, although liberalism has allowed for more gay and lesbian situation comedies and movies, where homosexuals can prove themselves to be just as good at total obedience to capital as any other "minority" group. A popular US television show in the late 1990s and early millennium, *Will & Grace*, portrayed its principal gay characters as bourgeois liberals whose main complaints were personal frustrations about

---

Ethics of Queer Life (Harvard University Press, 2000).

127 Fraser (Routledge, 1997), Cornell (Routledge, 1993), Guattari (Semiotext(e), 2001).

128 Federici, Silvia, *Revolution at Point Zero: Housework, Reproduction, and Feminist Struggle* (PM Press, 2012).

keeping a clean apartment and the superficiality of clothing, social status, and home decor. Any feminist movement that aims to demonstrate the happy felicity between all women and all gays and lesbians with the existing society, that aims to demonstrate their perfect compatibility, is a feminism that has nothing to offer communism. We naturally prefer Guattari's vision in "Becoming-Woman," where the subterranean existence of sexual minorities, and their rhizomatic capacities, is perceived as a real threat to the logic of capital – because it is.

To better grasp the relation of capital to human sexuality, we might consider, as just one measure, internet pornography statistics. In the US, internet pornography generates more revenue than all the revenues of the NFL, Major League Baseball and NBA sports franchises combined.[129] The pornography industry has larger revenues than Microsoft, Google, Amazon, eBay, Yahoo, Apple and Netflix combined.[130] The precarious communist makes no puritanical objection to pornography. These statistics are not invoked for the purposes of condemning pornography, or of defending some moral fabric. Rather, these facts are invoked to expose the colonization of human sexuality by capital, how much money is made in a methodically private – *indeed a secret and denied* – economy of sexual desire.

The meaning and complexity of marriage cannot be given any structural explanation through class analysis. Marx went too far in his generalizations about "bourgeois marriage," and couldn't foresee the assimilation of liberal feminist demands into bourgeois, heterosexual marriages.[131] Like capitalism, marriage has proven more dynamic and flexible than the structural analysis had indicated. In other words, marriage can survive innumerable permutations, and even get much-needed reinvigorations from recombination, as can be seen with the movement for same-gender marriage. Many people blockaded from marriage want to get in, which is inadvertently good news for the tradition of marriage because it helps to guarantee the indefinite lifespan of the institution, i.e., more people wanting and

---

129 Cited at http://www.gulfbreezenews.com/news/2011-07-21/Opinion/Porn_epidemic_threatens_countrys_moral_fabric.html (Accessed, 12/28/2012).

130 Ropelato, Jerry, "Internet Pornography Statistics" cited at http://internet-filter-review.toptenreviews.com/internet-pornography-statistics.html (Accessed, 12/28/2012). Also see, Hedges, Chris, *Empire of Illusion: The End of Literacy and the Triumph of the Spectacle* (Nation Books, 2009), especially Chapter II.

131 Marx, op. cit., p. 28.

seeking to be married. Feminist and queer incursions into the domain of monogamous marriage are not the same as the abolitionist cause of ending marriage altogether. But, precarious communists are resolutely uninterested in standardizing an approach to the various problems of marriage. The problems of marriage cannot be solved programmatically or categorically, and for that very reason, they are problems that call for an autonomist politics that understands the necessity of making – and keeping – common cause with people of multifarious lifeways. As there is no precarious communist party, there is no party line on marriage.

Precarious communists have no faith in the official politics of nations, and cannot be chauvinistic patriots. The national identity of a communist is either an accident of birth or the result of migrations and movements made by other causes than nationalism.

Precarious communists hew close to cosmopolitanism, and there can be no doubt that the cosmopolitan hospitality discussed by Immanuel Kant, the cosmopolitan solidarity discussed by Jürgen Habermas, and the cosmopolitan education discussed by Martha Nussbaum capture much in the internationalist spirit of communism, both old and new.[132] But precarious communists maintain at least two reservations about cosmopolitanism (which means that we are also precarious cosmopolitans) for two distinct reasons: (1) First, precarious communists have anarchist sensibilities, which is to say that we are suspicious of all scaling-up and consider the liberatory prospects of de-scaling, or scaling down. (2) Second, precarious communists may engage in micropolitical projects of such a localized nature that neither patriotism nor cosmopolitanism is relevant to our work. For us, it is not at all true that precarious communists "must first of all acquire political supremacy, must rise to be the leading class of the nation," or that the precarious communist class "must constitute itself *the* nation," because autonomous movements are not coordinated by any cohesive agenda, cannot be coordinated as such, and have a healthy anarchist allergy to the trappings of moving through national channels.[133]

Of the crucial things that Marx underestimated, the resilience and significance of nationality and nationalism is chief among them. Capital and state continue to make important uses of nationalism

---

132 Kant (Cambridge University Press, 1999), Habermas (The MIT Press, 2001), Nussbaum (Beacon Press, 2002).

133 Marx, op. cit., p. 28.

and international distinctions, and patriotism continues to show its capacity to flare up in the midst of terrorism, war, and economic crisis. Many Germans and French have felt a bit less "European" in the context of the capitalist crisis of the Eurozone (the British are happy to have kept the Pound) and the richest members of the EU are less inclined to uphold any obligations to the peoples of Greece, Spain, and Italy. Years before, many Americans who had no visible patriotism on September 10, 2001, expressed an inflamed patriotism stoked by the following day's attacks that still remains tender today, over eleven years later. As it turns out, the growing freedom of commerce throughout the world market that characterizes the current phase of globalization appears to develop without overturning or erasing national and patriotic identities that continue to thrive and survive in political-economy. Analysts still speak incessantly of national economies as if the whole network of exchange relations, the global division of labor, and monetary and market interdependencies didn't exist.

What is the supremacy of the precariat, if any at all? The world's precarious people, as an entire collectivity, have no clear advantage over the defenders and beneficiaries of capital, despite their overwhelming numbers. There are innumerable internal differentiations within the world precariat, too many to make anything cohesive for them, aside from their generalized precarity. However, if we specify precarious communists in particular, we can at least identify a shared contention, a shared aspiration. If precarious communists have any starting advantage it will be seen in the readiness of our expectation that capitalism is ultimately unliveable, and our conscious desire for something else.

In the 21st century, nation-states are finally disproving themselves as the inevitable or ideal political forms, and the truth of the second great contention of anarchism is being borne out.[134] In so many ways, the 20th century has already substantiated the validity of the first and most defining anarchist contention. That is, the anarchist contention about the invariable corruptibility of centralized power and hierarchical governance was a hard conclusion to resist in the light of totalitarianism. Mussolini, Hitler, Stalin, Ceauşescu, and many others

---

134 The first great contention of anarchism regards the rejection of centralized, hierarchical power, especially (but not only) pertaining to state power. The second great contention of anarchism regards the scale of the human community and the importance of self-rule over and against representation.

contributed to the effective devastation of good faith in hierarchical and authoritarian power structures. And now, few remain who could reasonably accept the notion of a temporary and withering proletarian dictatorship. Trusting one's government is a kind of universal joke, and this has been true for a long time. But, still alive well into the 21st century, another old mythology persists, that of capitalist representative democracy. Anarchists have for a long time pointed to the impossibility of the paradoxical notion of "representative democracy," arguing that representation is established in lieu of democracy, in fact, that representation is established deliberately to prevent democracy from taking place, safeguarding power. Anarchists from Charlotte Wilson and Errico Malatesta, to Fredy Perlman and David Graeber have argued this point well.[135] And, recent upheavals such as the "Arab Spring" (particularly the second wave of contestation against Mohamed Morsi in 2012), Occupy Wall Street, and the Greek and Spanish revolts are now removing the last stubborn obstacles to the vindication of anarchism's critical contention about political representation. Anarchist critique may well have needed 200 years to demonstrate its profundity, but these vindications (especially now, of the second great contention) are well underway. This will not make us one and all anarchists. Everyone is a bit of an anarchist, just as everyone should be, but anarchist recommendations have never been as good as their criticisms, and some anarchist positions have been ideologized to the point of pathology. For a properly serious reflection on anarchism, see Part III, Section 3, below.

Arguments against communism made from a religious or ideological standpoint (and there are great similarities between these standpoints), are quite absurd, but cannot be passed over in silence. Marx did not adequately attend to the difference and distance between ideology and philosophy. He continued, well after *The German Ideology*, to think of ideology and philosophy as a kind of tautology. To the contrary, we must always point out the differences between communism as ideology and communist philosophy.[136]

Marx's materialism made his own atheism an obvious and necessary conclusion. Marx might have liked the anti-theism of Christopher

---

135 Wilson (Freedom Press, 2000), Malatesta (Freedom Press, 2005), Perlman (Factory School, 2007), Graeber (AK Press, 2009).

136 I clarify these distinctions in *Spectacular Capitalism* (Minor Compositions/Autonomedia, 2011), pp. 12-29, and Chapter 3.

Hitchens, and certainly would have appreciated the popular atheist challenges of Sam Harris, Richard Dawkins, Peter Singer, and Daniel Dennett. What would have rightfully perplexed Marx is the fact that these critics of religion make no critique of capitalism (Peter Singer comes closest to such a critique, but does not have any problem with capitalism per se), and espouse a materialist science that claims, at least implicitly, capitalism as an ally.[137] The materialism of the new atheist or anti-theist wave of books and debates appears to accept capitalism as an irreversible and satisfactory fact of the world. Communism is treated as just another religious faith worthy of a similar scorn as Christianity, or, for the theistic side of the argument, as an example of why the absence of God is so dangerous.

Marx was right to declare that "[t]he ruling ideas of each age have ever been the ideas of its ruling class."[138] It is amazing that the scientific atheists and anti-theists of today's "new atheism" can so elegantly impale the religious pathologies of Christians, Muslims, and Jews, and yet find no pathological religiosity in their own continued faith in capitalism, which they take for granted far more uncritically than their opponents in the religious world have taken for granted the existence of God. At least the faithful theological scholars have been engaged in the consideration of arguments *for* and *against* the existence and goodness of God, or have had to rationalize their belief with philosophy or with history, or with capitulations to holy texts. For the faithful capitalist, on the other hand, it is not clear that the question of the continued existence or goodness of capitalism is ever actively asked. Indeed, "belief" in capitalism is not placed on the order of faith, but rather, on the order of accepting the immediate facts of the world, on the order of observing the color of the sky or the wetness of the water.

This point is critical. It is no longer the case that atheism and communism go together logically or inevitably. Marx insisted that religious faith served the capitalist world order and that atheism would serve the communists. But atheism can be, and has been, made to serve capital too. For many atheists, capitalism is a relatively unproblematic feature of the natural world of human beings, and while economic crises can be studied with scientific rigor, these economic crises are just like the environmental crises of earthquakes and tornadoes;

---

137 See, for example, Singer, Peter, *Practical Ethics: Second Edition* (Cambridge University Press, 1993), Chapter 8.

138 Marx, op. cit., p. 29.

that is, economic crises are studied only to be understood, and not to throw into question the viability of the system that gives rise to them.

Ideas do not always follow, or keep even pace with, the changing conditions of existence. Human imagination has been one of the biggest challenges to Marx's materialism. Imagination is not ideology, just as ideology is not philosophy, even though all three (imagination, philosophy, ideology) are powers of human thought. The ideational content of world religions was originally a great feat of human imagination, to be able to imagine a world that is not one's present world, to think through metaphysical origins stories imbued with moral and ethical teachings. But for all the subsequent generations who inherited their religion as an accident of birth, religion is far more ideological than imaginative. True, there are religious leaders and institutions, including, for example, the Vatican, that must always re-imagine religion in order to make old traditions speak to the future. And, religion as ideology is susceptible to philosophy, which can be seen whenever one throws the presuppositions of one's inherited religiosity into question. It is necessary to recognize that religion can be imaginative, ideological, or philosophical. A critique of capitalism and its culture often comes from synagogues, mosques, and churches: we could speak of the critique of pathological consumption, the ethical obligation to others (i.e., Hegel's notion of *Sittlichkeit*), or liberation theology. This is not to say that precarious communists must have some specific use for religion, but rather, that we cannot adopt a categorical rejection of all religiosity, and that we cannot treat all religion as equally preposterous from some unitary atheist perspective.

Marx's dialectical understanding of human history helps us to imagine the erasure of the current conditions of life by the emergence of new demands and new conditions of life. Marx sees a history in which the ancient religions were defeated and replaced by Christianity, and then, in the context of 18th century enlightenment, when Christianity loses ground to rationalism. Two points are worth noting here. First, much from the ancient world religions was absorbed into Christianity, and much of Christianity was absorbed into rationalism, so these transitions are, to say the very least, variegated and contaminated, each new development carrying much of the previous incarnations within it. Second, what did rationalism give way to? Is this how we arrive at postmodernity, by way of rationalism's giving way to a postmodern critique of reason and rational choice? We can see its beginnings already in Max Horkheimer's "The End of Reason."[139] Has rationalism given way to irrationalism, or perhaps, it is simply to ideology, which is both rational and irrational at the same time. Ideology is rational inasmuch as it enables us to rationalize the world, and provides us with a practical worldview that helps us to interpret events and to make sense of our place in the world. Ideology is irrational inasmuch as it functions without its philosophical precursors, that is, that people end up utilizing and embodying worldviews that they themselves did not think through. The conservatism of their parents has determined their own conservatism, for example, and without any separate or serious philosophical consideration, the question on every policy or political proposal is always to ask what a conservative must do.

But in light of the point about dialectical contaminations, the ideological and irrational dimensions of everyday life today contain within them more than a few traces of world religions and enlightenment rationalism. Dialectical change does not result in one state of total clarity or another. Dialectics makes mud. The transition from one state of affairs to another is always very muddy, and no antithesis is ever fully, or cleanly, triumphant. This is why we are able to speak honestly about Lenin and the "communist" revolution as not exactly a total negation of an industrial capitalist lifeworld (which did not yet exist in Russia), and as not being communism victoriously, clearly, or cleanly.[140]

Marx repeats his central claim: "The history of all past society has consisted in the development of class antagonisms, antagonisms that assumed different forms at different epochs."[141] This claim cannot be gainsaid. The problem is not its truth, but its centrality within Marx's system. Antagonisms are always present in human history, and their

---

139 Horkheimer, Max, "The End of Reason," Studies in Philosophy and Social Sciences, Vol. IX (1941) cited in *The Essential Frankfurt School Reader* (Continuum, 2002).

140 This is why honest assessments cannot but confess the truth of those contemporaneous critiques of the Russian case written by Antonio Gramsci and Cornelius Castoriadis. See Gramsci's "The Revolution Against *Capital*" in *The Antonio Gramsci Reader: Selected Writings 1916 – 1935* (New York University Press, 2000) and Castoriadis' "The Relations of Production in Russia" in *Cornelius Castoriadis: Political and Social Writings: Volume 1, 1946-1955: From the Critique of Bureaucracy to the Positive Content of Socialism* (University of Minnesota Press, 1988).

141 Marx, op. cit., p. 29.

changing nature *does* define the main disputes of each epoch. But antagonisms are not the only unit of analysis for historical understanding, nor should they be. For example, the absence of antagonisms is of equal or greater importance. The history of subordination and acquiescence can also be told, as can the history of alienation, the history of anxiety, and the history of certain phases of dominant ideology.

It is true that exploitation and social stratification are consistent facts of every era, but no communist today can reasonably look forward to "the total disappearance of class antagonisms."[142] Non-ideological communism is too precarious to count on totalities of any kind.

On some occasions, Marx wrote directly about "the communist revolution," which must today be replaced with a more pluralistic and precarious term.[143] "Communist insurrections" are the more likely (though not the only possible) eventuality, and could involve riots and other social upheavals that throw into question existing property relations and the logic of capital, among other things.

But let us have done with "communist" impediments to communism.

We cannot proclaim the first, second, or third steps in making revolution, but we can nonetheless be more concrete about the demands of precarious communists.

Jacques Rancière wrote a beautiful little book called *Hatred of Democracy*, in which he theorizes democracy in line with anarchist conceptions of a directly and self-governing demos. "Strictly speaking, democracy is not a form of State. It is always beneath and beyond these forms. Beneath, insofar as it is the necessarily egalitarian, and necessarily forgotten, foundation of the oligarchic state. Beyond, insofar as it is the public activity that counteracts the tendency of every State to monopolize and depoliticize the public sphere. Every State is oligarchic."[144] Rancière argues that those who are the most vocal proponents of democracy today tend to be the most fearful of its actual emergence in the world. The most prominent defenders of democracy tend to be defenders of the State, procedural politics, contestation by elections alone, in short, the present state of affairs. Those who proclaim to love democracy the most secretly harbor the greatest

---

142 Ibid.
143 Ibid.
144 Rancière, Jacques, *Hatred of Democracy* (Verso Books, 2006), p. 71.

contempt for the idea of everyday people in direct and assertive control of their lives. When precarious communists engage in a battle over democracy, it is not to establish democracy of one form or another, not to make a so-called democratic state, but rather, to destroy the conceit of self-proclaimed democracies everywhere, pointing out the hostile incompatibilities of capitalism and democracy.

The precariat has no political supremacy because political power rests on capital and not on sheer numbers of people. So the precariat cannot take the state, or organize itself as the ruling class. But the state and the ruling class do become more precarious the more that the whole social order does. In 2011 and 2012 we saw this in Egypt, in 2012 we saw this in Syria, and in 2013 we saw this in Turkey and Brazil. The precariat can and must, therefore, share its precarity, undermining the security of the least precarious. The chief power of the precariat is its ability to make the systems responsible for its precarity aware of their own uncertain future.

Assuming the political supremacy of the proletariat, Marx allowed for the temporary use of despotic means to reverse the backwards conditions of bourgeois production, to safeguard revolutionary changes, and to help create the conditions under which despotic means are no longer necessary. But precarious communists do not need to worry about the uses of despotism. We are incapable of despotism because we have no grand plan to carry out, we are unskilled in bureaucracy, and would seek the negation of any supreme power as a matter of dialectics, distrust, or subversive inclination. Precarious communists know too much history to look for answers in state power. As has been discussed, we have healthy anarchist sensibilities. Our capabilities are for autonomy, not for autocracy. Precarious communists are autonomists.

The concrete measures of precarious communists are different everywhere.

Nevertheless, some general aspirations may be outlined.

1. According to the logic of capital, all land, natural and human resources and every inhabitable, usable space – indeed, all of space and time – is either private or subject to privatization. The logic of capital is not the logic of shared interest and public well-being. (When we say "public," we do not mean "public institutions of governance.") We pursue alternative logics to the logic of capital.

2. We understand that gross disparities of income and property are endemic to capitalism, and that practically, they translate into gross disparities of opportunity within the existing society. While precarious communists oppose the logic of capital, and thus the society organized by that logic, we can demand reversals of disparity within the limits of existing society in the name of "damage control" in the here and now. This only means that we do not limit our demands to the greatest aspirations of communist desire in the promise for some uncertain future.

3. For too many, wealth, property, and opportunity (and the lack thereof) are accidents of birth, determined by class, inheritance, and luck. Precarious communists understand the fact that most infants are established at birth as rich or poor, that upward mobility is a demonstrable lie, and that the avenues facing the very young are either opened or closed from the start, not determined by personal responsibility. If we would speak of injustice, the radical disadvantage of human beings from infancy is a noncontroversial case. On normative grounds, we take sides with those on the losing end of this equation.

4. We cannot effectively punish or pre-empt the autonomous actions of others. We can of course criticize the arguments and actions of precarious communists, with respect for the manifold of communist desire, and with respect for the destructive and constructive aspirations of communism. For example, is there any doubt that communists will dispute these enumerated aspirations? On the other hand, we seek to criticize capitalism with the comportment of negation in as many diverse and creative ways as possible, including by ways of revolt.

5. Contestatory presence (occupy when and where uninvited) and contestatory absence (strike when and where expected) are good oppositional principles. Other oppositional principles of non-working and other-doing can be imagined and explored. John Holloway defines other-doing as "an activity

that is not determined by money, an activity that is not shaped by the rules of power."[145]

6. De-privatize (or publicize) the means of communication, everywhere opposing control by commercial interests of planning and content. Familiar modalities such as social media, alternative media, and even culture jamming are inadequate because they presuppose their own marginality and are most effectively utilized by a small coterie of celebrities. The catalogue of subaltern and subversive cultural and artistic projects discussed by Brian Holmes in his *Unleashing the Collective Phantoms: Essays in Reverse Imagineering* points out more promising directions.[146] The democratization of communication depends upon new precedents of thought and action. Consider a prominent case of the backwards logic of social media: If Facebook depends on its users to thrive and survive then Mark Zuckerberg depends on the world of users for his fortunes. Instead, when Facebook became "publicly tradeable," investors were asked to purchase company shares in order to convert some share of the company's wealth into their legal property. Inasmuch as Zuckerberg's wealth depends upon the voluntary activities of more than one billion Facebook users worldwide, and inasmuch as this voluminous active base is the necessary precondition for Facebook's exchange-value, Facebook users are, in fact, Zuckerberg's unpaid workforce. We should consider the expropriation in that relationship. According to the logic of capital, one might retort: "But he provides a free service!" That is an inverted logic. It is the users who provide a free service to Zuckerberg. In fact, Zuckerberg could be seen as an iconic case of the "free rider." Zuckerberg gives nothing for free. If Facebook was free, how could it have happened that, as of March 2012, Forbes Magazine valued Zuckerberg's net worth at $17.5 billion? Forbes lists the source of Zuckerberg's wealth as "self-made," but Zuckerberg's partially self-made technological innovation made him no money at all – it was the voluntary active base

---

145 Holloway, John, *Crack Capitalism* (Pluto Press, 2010), p. 3.
146 Holmes, Brian, *Unleashing the Collective Phantoms: Essays in Reverse Imagineering* (Autonomedia, 2008).

of Facebook users who accomplished that for him. Without those one billion plus, Zuckerberg and company would not command a voluntarily populated and autonomously updating database of so much of the world population. In a certain sense, we possess a latent power over all those fortunes, which could be exercised, for example, in a kind of general cyber-strike, a mass closure of accounts. To be clear, I am not suggesting anything particularly malignant or offensive about Facebook. I am not suggesting that such a strike would accomplish any concrete goal (although, under imaginable circumstances, it might). Technological phases have histories, and the terms of this example can and will change. What is true about Facebook in the present discussion has nothing to do with Facebook substantively or intrinsically. The example is given to illustrate the formal inversion of communist logic in existing social media, and the lines of thought required to reverse the privatization of communication.

7. Human production and social organization are today capable of understanding ecology. Following this, it is increasingly necessary to counterpose the logic of social-ecology to the logic of capital, to consider their ultimate incompatibilities, and not to accept the new mythologies of "green" capitalism. This can be done in an anarchist way, or following the analysis and recommendations of Murray Bookchin or James O'Connor, but it need not follow any such blueprint or thinker.[147] Other examples include agriculture in Cuba after the collapse of the Soviet Union and, on a smaller scale, community gardening.

8. Creativity outside of (and against) "work" is a human right, and should be treated as such regardless of the law.

9. Free education for all children and adults, that old anarchist and communist refrain, must be defended, and it is an idea and practice under greater threat today than at any point in human history. Educational planning must not be determined by what

---

147 See Bookchin, Murray, *Social Ecology and Communalism* (AK Press, 2007) and O'Connor, James, *Natural Causes: Essays in Ecological Marxism* (The Guilford Press, 1998).

kind of education will make the graduate the most money. At its best, education cultivates other values and other-doing.

10. There are resources for all of the above. We do not regard "capital" as synonymous with "resources." But scarcity is one of the most cherished lies of capitalist mythology. There are always adequate financial resources for the projects of capital, especially for wars and bank bailouts. If our aspirations seem impossible, that is all the more reason to pursue them. Let us leave what is readily possible to the efforts of liberal reformers. They do not need a manifesto.

This list is by no means exhaustive. *It is not even ideal.* It is a détournement of Marx's list. In Marx's list, certain tasks were concretely given to the communist state, including taxation, confiscation of bourgeois property, banking, communication, and transportation. It is in the paragraph following this list that Marx explains his famous notion of the withering state:

> When, in the course of development, class distinctions have disappeared, and all production has been concentrated in the hands of a vast association of the whole nation, the public power will lose its political character. Political power, properly so called, is merely the organized power of one class for oppressing another. If the proletariat during its contest with the bourgeoisie is compelled, by the force of circumstances, to organize itself as a class; if, by means of a revolution, it makes itself the ruling class, and, as such sweeps away by force the old conditions of production, then it will, along with these conditions, have swept away the conditions for the existence of class antagonisms, and of classes generally, and will thereby have abolished its own supremacy as a class.[148]

Here, Marx is arguing that the proletariat may need to seize the public institutions of power (i.e., government) in order to ensure the implementation of those tasks that the state must carry out, and also,

---

148 Marx, op. cit., p. 31.

in order to keep down counterrevolutionary forces of the domestic and international bourgeoisie. But the aspirations of communism, for Marx, could not possibly end in the tenuous state of revolutionary insecurity, and so he imagined a state that would help to create the conditions under which the state would no longer need to exist. If the state, as Marx says above, "is merely the organized power of one class for oppressing another," and if the end of class oppression is a classless society, then Marx cannot be calling for a permanent state. It is logically impossible. Thus, Marx insists on a transitory and withering state. This is central to the complexity of Marx's theory of state power. The anarchists of the 19th century were already worried about Marx's theory of the withering state, especially Mikhail Bakunin.[149] Honest Marxists today must confess that the anarchist anxiety about state power was vindicated in the 20th century, not Marx's hopeful contentions. This is also why the communist currents of the 21st century must be precarious.

---

149 See Bakunin, Mikhail, *Statism and Anarchy* (Cambridge University Press, 1990), p. 179.

III.

Excurses

1.
Principles

A. DIGNITY

IS THERE A PERSON ANYWHERE WHO DOES NOT WANT DIGNITY? WE ARE suspicious of universal principles, and we know that dignity may be defined differently by different people. Some men continue to think that patriarchy is necessary to their dignity. The wife may be a feminist who denies that the man's dignity is contingent upon her subordination, but she too wants dignity. What is dignity?

The word and concept have problematic moorings, encrusted from the 13th century with connections to privilege, nobility, and social rank. But its more general conceptualization includes notions of worthiness, fitness, recognition, and respect. A human person wants her worth to be recognized, wants what she does to be properly appreciated by others, wants to do what she feels most fit to do, and this whole constellation of things necessary for human dignity depends upon self-respect. If a person has little or no self-respect, then she cannot feel her worth, she will not trust the affirmative recognition of others, she will not understand what she is fit to do, and she may not know how to distinguish practical necessity from actual desire. In this way, human dignity is inextricably linked to human psychology.

The subjective basis of a demand for dignity is, in another way, what makes the affective position of the undignified so powerful. If a person does not feel that they have their dignity, no one can tell them otherwise. Dignity is a strange kind of property. Whether or not one has their dignity can only be assessed on an affective level. The Mexican government could not tell the Mayan population of Chiapas in the mid-1990s that they were well respected and being treated in accordance with their worth. When white US football fans insist that their Native American team mascots are meant to dignify, and not to degrade, their claim is totally irrelevant. What matters is only the extent to which Native Americans *feel* dignified or not by the icons. If the "housewife" is reassured by her husband that she is doing what she is most fit to do, and is duly appreciated, rewarded, and recognized, one question still remains: How does she feel about it? The Chick-fil-A restaurant chain cannot claim that they are all for the dignity of homosexuals while publicly expressing their confident belief, grounded in the bible, that gays and lesbians are destined for the lake of fire. If human dignity means anything to you, then you cannot defer the question to those who are in the position of reassuring the ones they offend that they should not be offended. If we make the assumption of self-respect, then only the affectations of the person can be the measure of her dignity.

The problem is that we cannot assume self-respect. The precariat is anxious, and from a clinical perspective, anxiety is very closely related with depression and a lack of confidence. This feature of capitalist societies today has been deeply explored by Zygmunt Bauman (2007), Paul Virilio (2012), Franco Berardi (2009), and Paolo Virno (1996).[150] These authors analyse the condition of our uncertainty, precarity, fear, and disenchantment with such depth and precision, that their works provide the substantive basis for understanding the problems facing human dignity today.

We shall only touch on a couple of points from these sources here.

---

150 See Bauman, Zygmunt, *Liquid Times: Living in an Age of Uncertainty* (Polity Press, 2007); Virilio, Paul, *The Administration of Fear* (Semiotext(e), 2012); Berardi, Franco, *The Soul at Work: From Alienation to Autonomy* (Semiotext(e), 2009); Virno, Paolo, "The Ambivalence of Disenchantment" in *Radical Thought in Italy: A Potential Politics* (University of Minnesota Press, 1996).

Bauman suggests that "[f]ear is arguably the most sinister of the de-mons nesting in the open societies of our time. But it is the insecurity of the present and uncertainty about the future that hatch and breed the most awesome and least bearable of our fears."[151] If we have no se-curity today, and no certainty about tomorrow, and if this causes us an awesome and almost-unbearable fear, then the demand for a dignified life is not easily on the horizon. We might first worry about achieving some level of security and certainty, which are not the same thing as dig-nity. Security and certainty may be more pressing than dignity from the standpoint of immediate practical needs, but they guarantee nothing by way of dignity. Pornography, for example, is among the least precarious industries, and among the most anonymous and secretive. Why? There is a lot of security and certainty in the present and future of the pornog-raphy industry, and its precarity mainly derives from the possibility of regulative legislation. But those involved in every level of its production, distribution, and consumption, prefer anonymity, pseudonyms, or out-right secrecy, on the basis of a shared consensus – even internal to the industry – about the dignity of the work.[152]

Marx had a rather strong understanding of the importance of dig-nity, which he articulated early on in his *Economic and Philosophic Manuscripts of 1844*. "A *forcing-up of wages* (disregarding all other dif-ficulties, including the fact that it would only be by force, too, that the higher wages, being an anomaly, could be maintained) would therefore be nothing but *better payment for the slave*, and would not conquer either for the worker or for labour their human status and dignity."[153] This is illustrated in any case where, when the content of one's everyday life activity is felt to be undignified, a raise in wages may be welcome for practical purposes, but does nothing to amelio-rate the problem of dignity.

---

151 Bauman, Zygmunt, *Liquid Times: Living in an Age of Uncertainty* (Polity Press, 2007), p. 26.

152 This issue is explored rather well in "Chapter II: The Illusion of Love" in Chris Hedges' *Empire of Illusion: The End of Literacy and the Triumph of Spectacle* (Na-tion Books, 2009). Also, it should be noted that when I speak of the security and certainty of pornography as an industry, I am not speaking of the so-called "porn stars," for they are precarious and exploited in too many ways to catalogue here. I am speaking of the industry from the point of view of its continued existence, its capitalist security, and the permanence of its consumer base.

153 Marx, Karl, *Economic and Philosophic Manuscripts of 1844*, (Dover Publications, 2007), p. 81.

Paolo Virno has done one of the best jobs of diagnosing the prob-lems of a generalized disenchantment. The disenchantment Virno de-scribes creates obstacles to, and sets the stage for, dignity's revolt.[154] Virno writes:

> The phantasmagoria of abstract possibilities in which the opportunist acts is colored by *fear* and secretes *cyni-cism*. It contains infinite negative and privative chances, infinite threatening "opportunities." Fears of particular dangers, if only virtual ones, haunt the workday like a mood that cannot be escaped. This fear, however, is trans-formed into an operational requirement, a special tool of the trade. Insecurity about one's place during periodic innovation, fear of losing recently gained privileges, and anxiety over being "left behind" translate into flexibility, adaptability, and a readiness to reconfigure oneself.[155]

Precarious workers have no choice but to become more opportu-nistic, and they do so with a good deal of fear and cynicism. Virno sees that this comportment perfectly suits capital, because the opportunist must become increasingly flexible and adaptable in order to safeguard gains, to be poured into any mold required by his or her employer, and thus to hopefully be retained indefinitely into the future. The situation Virno describes is dissuasive to demanding dignity. In that context, a demand or expectation for dignity would seem to indicate inflexibility, or a reluctance to reconfigure oneself, and so the happi-ness of the precarious worker is indefinitely relegated to the realm of the risky and impractical.

But Virno sees the other side of this. He points out that the whole assemblage of features of everyday life at work "make that situation vis-ible as an irreversible fact on whose basis conflict and revolt might also be conceived."[156] Thus, Virno speaks of worker defection and exodus. Occupation is another modality of revolt, an alternative oppositional

---

154 The term "dignity's revolt" comes from the title of an essay by John Holloway, which describes the Zapatista revolt in the context of demands for dignity. See Chapter 8 of *Zapatistas! Reinventing Revolution in Mexico*, edited by John Hol-loway and Eloina Peláez (Pluto Press, 1998).

155 Virno, Paolo, "The Ambivalence of Disenchantment," in *Radical Thought in Italy: A Potential Politics* (University of Minnesota Press, 1996), p.17.

156 Ibid., p. 33.

logic to that of flight (i.e., strike, defection, and exodus). Despite capitalist dissuasion, dignity is capable of revolt. No one wants a life without dignity, and a prolonged acceptance of the absence of dignity, or its prolonged suppression, is always maintained against countervailing social and psychological forces, possibly even, against a universal human aspiration.

B. AUTONOMY

Long before the tumultuous decade in Italy, "autonomia" was given its meanings in Greece in the 17th century. The word's etymological and conceptual content have always indicated the subject, pointed toward the self, and have always implicated a kind of independence of the subject from external coercions, including those of law, of state, and of the expectations (including habit, custom, and culture) of everyday life. Autonomy rests on the subjective position of the self ("auto"), and isolates the human will, whether individual or general, as central to the meaning of freedom. In many ways, the question of the self is the question of the will. *Does freedom exist if one is only free to do those things that one does not want to do?* If you cannot do what you really desire to do, for example, we might say that you lack autonomy. Autonomous action follows the will, and even where doing so is quite difficult, say, because one does not even know what one really wants, autonomous action cannot negate the will of the subject. This is because the maximum of autonomy is self-governance.

Following this, we could say that autonomy was the overarching and central theme of struggles against colonization throughout the 20th century. Decolonization, and its theoretical counterparts in postcolonial studies, is fundamentally about autonomy. It is critical here to note that autonomy can be communist, in the sense of a self-governing community acting in the interests of its own will, against the opposing will of the colonial power. In this way, decolonization is a movement of communist autonomy, autonomy of/for a particular human community.

Despite Antonio Negri's many decades of important and influential work to rethink class and revolution beyond Marx's own lexicon, Negri could report the following frustration: "As recently as 2003, during a European Forum for the movements in Paris, I had to debate with an English Trotskyist, who spoke of the working class as though we were still in the nineteenth century and, of course, of the revolution, as though the twentieth had never existed."[157] This shows us that the working class has been ideologized within communist discourses to the point where communists have scarcely noticed that the working class, as the inexorable revolutionary subject, does not exist. Indeed, Marx's more "scientific" articulations did identify the working class as an objectively real revolutionary subject-in-process. The objective existence of the proletariat as such could be measured by empirical analysis, and its behavior as a transnational class could be explained within the context of the class analysis. Negri uses the notion of autonomy to develop new ways of theorizing Marxism beyond Marx's fixation on the proletariat as the revolutionary subject position.

Autonomy implicates governance in the sense of "self-governance," not as external institutions governing the self from outside of or even against the self. Therefore, autonomy has some necessary implications for politics. Negri explains this as follows: "Our problem is one of *establishing the autonomy of the political - not where the political is emancipated from the social, but where the political entirely and independently reassumes within itself the social...* In the theoretical situation in which we are acting, *the political* is not, in fact, an abstraction of the social, but is, rather, a *social abstraction*. The political is communication; it is the symbolic; it is the material which establishes social, productive cooperation and allows the latter to reproduce itself and produce value."[158]

In other words, autonomy does not separate the social from the political, making each side autonomous from the other. Instead, we understand the political as something that emanates from the social, and occurs throughout the social body. The political is not merely legitimized by the social (as in the conceit of institutions of "representative democracy"), but rather, is carried out by and though the social directly. In earlier generations of political theory, including in the works of Hobbes, Locke, and Rousseau, political institutions were abstract embodiments of the social, as, for example, could be seen in the frontispiece illustration of *Leviathan*. Today, we must finally understand that the political forms of the state possess a symbolic value

---

157 Negri, Antonio, *The Politics of Subversion: A Manifesto for the Twenty-First Century*, p. X.
158 Ibid., p. 146.

or embody general sentiments, which are communicated and reified throughout the social, as one can see during any national election cycle. The state is one location where the political becomes readily visible, where we can see political phenomena in the world, but it is neither the formative nor substantive location of politics. The autonomy of the political from the social, the idea of the political as above and beyond the social, rests ultimately on the imagination of the social. But we are also capable of new realizations, new values, and most critically, new self-recognitions of ourselves as subjects. What this means is that autonomy depends upon particular self-recognitions, which are often expressed in and by social movements, riots, rebellions, various moments of exodus or occupation, and in other creative modes of revolt. In this way, Negri is an autonomist thinker who *does not* theorize autonomy as post-political or non-political, but rather, as counter-political.

In regards to the relation of autonomy to the will, Franco Berardi unpacks the general meaning well: "In the framework of autonomous thought the concept of social class is redefined as an investment of social desire, and that means culture, sexuality, refusal of work... In this view autonomy means that social life does not depend only on the disciplinary regulation imposed by economic power, but also depends on the internal displacement, shifts, settlings and dissolutions that are the process of the self-composition of living society; struggle, withdrawal, alienation, sabotage, and lines of flight from the capitalist system of domination."[159]

With Berardi's definition in mind, we can say that autonomy relates to the will in that it shifts attention from a purely economic self-understanding to the psycho-social understanding of our desires, including our sexual desires, and even the desire not to work. Within the context of wanting to be a saboteur, or wanting to flee from the everyday life of capitalist work and from the logic of capital (the latter of which extends just as much to the unemployed), the question of what one wants (what one wants to be or wants to do) is unavoidable. We can know that we want dignity, and we know what dignity feels like, but we do not want dignity for its own sake. If we want a dignified life it is because we want our own lives, we do not want to place our entire life in the service of capital, into the ownership of money.

159 Berardi, *Precarious Rhapsody: Semiocapitalism and the Pathologies of the Post-alpha Generation* (Minor Compositions/Autonomedia, 2009), pp. 74-75.

This is indeed a question of human will, for our wills, individual and collective, cannot be left in abeyance forever.

It bears repeating that autonomy neither abides by nor is nurtured by the logic of capital. Capital only allows for autonomy in the service of its accumulative aspirations. You can do what you will on holiday, assuming that you have the money to do what you will, but you have to come back soon, as workers always say "much too soon." But you come back nonetheless because you understand the nature of your precarity and its practical stakes, and you know that there are others who do not take all of their vacation days and who are therefore deemed "more flexible" or "more hard-working." If you are among the unemployed, the demands of capital outstrip all other aspects of your will, except for the will to live, that most primordial bit of will that you follow up to the point of total resignation or suicide. In short, self-recognition and self-realization are pursued within the limits of capitalist commitments, contingencies, and arrangements, that is to say, mainly within the space of an endangered species called "free time." In this setting, autonomy remains for us a principle and a possibility, but is more often than not, a casualty.[160]

C. ASSOCIATION

What is association, how does it relate to sociality, and what does it do?

First, we consider the meaning from the 16th century, very generally, the action of coming together. Involved in this conception are therefore multiplicity and activation. Associations do not passively exist. They form and dissipate by way of action and inaction, respectively. They are agonistic in the conventional sense, voluntary eventualities created by coming together for certain purposes. Associations are thus purposive, as in the 17th century, the concept of association came to mean specifically a body of persons with a common purpose. Actually existing associations in the world depend upon a formative "mental connection," through which we associate for specific purposes, in the name or the idea of something. Since association is agonistic,

---

160 For a more thorough analysis of the antagonistic relation of capital to autonomy, see Gilman-Opalsky, Richard, "Beyond the Old Virtue of Struggle: Autonomy, Talent, and Revolutionary Theory" (Rhizomes Journal, Number 24, 2012).

it includes the notion of a voluntary and cooperative action, and although people may associate on the basis of a feeling that they must now do so, that they are compelled to do so by material circumstances, they cannot be coerced into association. People can indeed be forcibly organized, unionized, incorporated, or otherwise thrown together against their wills. History is full of examples. But the key to differentiating association from such other modes of coming together is to understand association as a voluntary relation, not a relation of force.

Second, no formal institutions are necessary for association. Association is the substantive action of what Hannah Arendt and Jürgen Habermas theorize as the public sphere.[161] The voluntary agonistic collective and communicative action that creates the public sphere (a specifically political association) enables us to understand the total compatibility of association in general with autonomous action. What distinguishes association from the public sphere is that association is the broader term, and can indicate pre-political or non-political comings together. Thus, every public sphere is an association, but not every association is a public sphere. Most importantly, there must be some autonomy in order to associate.

In Article 20 of The Universal Declaration of Human Rights, lines (1) and (2) state: "Everyone has the right to freedom of peaceful assembly and association" and "No one may be compelled to belong to an association." Article 11 of the European Convention on Human Rights also protects the right to freedom of association. Thus, liberals have long understood that association is not a coerced relation, and also, that association is a human activity that governments might try to disallow. The liberal tradition views association as a human right, as a part of already-existing "democracy," whereas precarious communists see association as the modality through which collective expressions of disaffection against the existing state of affairs are made. In short, liberals view association as a means of legitimation, whereas precarious communists view association as a means of contestation, of the delegitimation of power. And there are other dimensions of association.

Association also functions on an affective level that cannot be overlooked. When a person is sick and locks themselves up from the

---

161 See Arendt, Hannah, *The Human Condition* (University of Chicago Press, 1958), and Habermas, Jürgen, *The Structural Transformation of the Public Sphere: An Inquiry into a Category of Bourgeois Society* (The MIT Press, 1989).

world, sometimes the sickness hangs on, and the isolation of quarantine grows deeper every day. The absence of sociality is felt in such moments, using Marx expression, as alienation from *species being*, from one's sense of what it means to be human. Sometimes, it doesn't take much to feel cut off from one's own self and from others. There are better examples than sickness, but everyone's been sick. Isolation in our world has given rise to a whole host of psycho-social maladies, diagnosed and treated on epidemic levels through psychotropic drugs. Depression and anxiety are closely related from the standpoint of clinical psychology and, as discussed previously (Part I. More or Less Anxious), Kristeva considers national depression as the social condition of feeling cut off from others, including from your closest friends and family. It is precisely within this context that association functions as a countervailing force to isolation. Within association, we find human solidarity, we find moments of its realization and expression. It is not much of a secret that activists often go to political demonstrations, not because they suffer the delusion that they are changing the world, but because they find human solidarity there that mitigates the sense of being alone. Radicals in academia attend small thematic conferences, partly to learn and to engage in peer-review, but also to make meaningful associations with others like them for informally therapeutic reasons.

Hikikomori is an interesting condition that has drawn the attention of countless scholars across many fields. The Japanese word itself means pulling inward, being confined, and refers to manifestations of acute social withdrawal. Hikikomori refers to the phenomenon of mostly adolescent and young adults who cannot handle human association, who reject all expected forms of sociality, and even seek out and defend their isolation. According to the Japanese government, there were 700,000 individuals living as hikikomori in 2010. But the government estimates 1.55 million people to be on the verge of becoming hikikomori.[162] The intensity of the cases of hikikomori varies, but in the most extreme cases, people remain in isolation for years or even decades.

The Japanese Ministry of Health, Labour and Welfare defines hikikomori as people who refuse to leave their house and who isolate

---

162 Hoffman, Michael, "Nonprofits in Japan help 'shut-ins' get out into the open" cited at The Japan Times (Online) at http://www.japantimes.co.jp/text/fd-20111009bj.html (Accessed, 12/28/2012).

themselves from society for a period exceeding six months.[163] Here, it is critical to see that association is not the same thing as society. Society, the social world outside, consists of a web of human relationality that can be both involuntary and purposeless. The comings together of human bodies in trains, shopping malls, traffic jams, schools, and workplaces is not agonistic in the sense of autonomous, voluntary, meaningful association. Thus, association is often absent in society, and the two can even be opposed, such that association mitigates the isolation of the social world. There is that famous saying about being alone in a crowd, also often experienced at parties or pubs, which has become the generalized condition of life in a privatized mass society. Loneliness is better remedied with association than with society. Society often exacerbates feelings of loneliness.

It is worth noting that hikikomori often starts out in the form of school refusals. The Japanese education system places high demands upon its youth, giving rise to extreme forms of anxiety. A multitude of expectations, and notably, an overarching emphasis on individuation and competition, accompanied with rote memorization of facts and figures for the purpose of passing entrance exams, leads young people to the breaking point of stress. In this way, hikikomori may be a defense mechanism, a retreat from the anxiety of the everyday life of young people in an increasingly competitive, individualistic, and precarious lifeworld. Predictably, the main disposition of clinical psychology toward hikikomori has been to integrate the isolated and the anxious into society, not to transform the competitive logic of the conditions that create it. Hikikomori is a Japanese term, but not an exclusively Japanese phenomenon. It has begun to show up in France.[164] In other countries, the same impulse can be found everywhere, in different forms, for example, in the social withdrawal of social media or in the world of gaming, which are perhaps more sustainable because they allow for an isolation interrupted by simulated associations that compensate for some of the affective deficits of society. The now-regular occurrence of mass killings in the US carried out

---

163 Itou, Junichirou, "Shkaiteki Hikikomori Wo Meguru Tiki Seisin Hoken Katudou No Guideline - Mental Health Activities in Communities for Social Withdrawal" (Tokyo: Ministry of Health, Labour and Welfare, 2010) cited at http://www.squidoo.com/japan-and-hikikomori (Accessed, 12/28/2012).

164 Gozlan, Marc, "Des cas d'hikikomori en France" in Le Monde, Science and Technology Section, 09 June, 2012, p. 3.

by profoundly disturbed young men who have opened fire in movie theaters (i.e., Colorado, 2012), shopping malls (i.e., Oregon, 2012), temples (i.e., Wisconsin, 2012) and schools (i.e., Connecticut, 2012) is not diagnosed as part of a generalized psychological crisis linked to an increasingly precarious lifeworld, but it should be. Looking at these killings as problems of gun control and/or as the failures of the mental health system are the prominent red herrings that relieve us of the burden of having to think much about the social system and its attendant pathologies.

The relationship of association to communism can now be approached more concretely. It is difficult to resist the clear resonances between disassociation and capitalism, on the one hand, and between our associational aspirations and the communist idea, on the other.

Jacques Camatte contrasted two possible meanings of *Gemeinwesen*. What Camatte refers to as the true *Gemeinwesen* is the really existing community of human persons, whereas the capitalist *Gemeinwesen* constructs a community of exchange relations which could even exist without the human person. "The question of alienation can only be treated exhaustively if linked with the question of *Gemeinwesen*... In fact, the concept of alienation implies the process, at once historical and contemporary, or, if you like, diachronic and synchronic, through which the human being (being for itself) becomes another being, who is not or who is no longer present as *Gemeinwesen*... He behaves, for example, as a worker... So at the beginning there are beings who dominate things; at the end things become beings."[165]

What, exactly, does Camatte mean, and how does this help us understand the relationship between association and communism? Beneath the idea of communism lies the idea of the human community, the commons, or the commune, and *Gemeinwesen*, the real human community, is the name given to actual embodiments of communist spirit. Camatte reads this conception of communism directly in Marx's texts, particularly in *Economic and Philosophic Manuscripts of 1844*, *Grundrisse*, and *Capital*. *Gemeinwesen*, in the communist sense, is the opposite of alienation and isolation, and therefore directly positions human association as an antidote. The human person, Camatte observes, becomes something other than herself, becomes a student, a waitress, a worker, a representative, she comes to be an active

---

165 Camatte, Jacques, *Capital and Community* (Prism Key Press, 2011), pp. 240-241.

representative of something or someone other than herself. Becoming (and with it, being) in the capitalist lifeworld means becoming/being operational within the community of capitalist exchange relations. Your lover or your closest friend knows who you are, but within everyday life, that is not your state of being. The sense of liberation one may experience at the end of the workday (before the next work-related seizure of consciousness) is understandable within the context of a movement from being-for-capital (i.e., as a worker), to another modality of being, being-for-itself, or being-for-some-other-doing.

In the example of hikikomori we could see very sharply that the normative expectations of everyday life call upon a mode of being that is not desirable to many young people, which they want to flee from, to radically reject (i.e., as hikikomori). Other, more widespread pathological behaviors of withdrawal, privatization, social anxiety, and depression, only strengthen this thesis. The problem is not human association per se, but rather, that a healthy and desirable form of human association is not easily available to those who most need an antidote to everyday alienation. Thus, in the case of hikikomori, as with other pathological forms of isolation, social withdrawal appears to be a more practical (and immediate) avenue than human association. In contrast, the communist discourse recommends associational defensive and offensive responses to alienation, that is, the pursuit and construction of real *Gemeinwesen*, instead of social withdrawal. Social withdrawal is not only dangerous for politics, for the health of the *demos*, but aids and abets privatization trends. Part of the problem is that personal acts of social withdrawal are far easier to carry out than the collective action of *Gemeinwesen*. Too often, therefore, *Gemeinwesen* is the last refuge of the disaffected.

Camatte writes of the communist aspiration for *Gemeinwesen* as follows: "Humanity will constitute itself in a collective being, the *Gemeinwesen*... communism is the affirmation of a being, the true *Gemeinwesen* of man. Direct democracy appears to be a means for achieving communism. However communism does not need such a mediation. It is not a question of having or of doing, but of being."[166] The central importance of a healthy mode of human association to Camatte's conception of communism is quite clear: Human association must be understood on the level of human being, of being human.

---

166 Camatte, Jacques, *The Selected Works of Jacques Camatte* (Prism Key Press, 2011), pp. 95-96.

In a world so obedient to capital, our collective being, the *Gemein-wesen*, scarcely has the space and time to express its self, because the nature of everyday life, of human relationality, has been so ruthlessly privatized.[167] Nonetheless, communist relationality cannot be totally extinguished for as long as human life persists, and thus the *Gemein-wesen* asserts itself in therapeutic human gatherings, whether planned or spontaneous, in the fleeting-yet-most-affirming moments of a life.

I have been drawing on Camatte for two reasons here. First, few thinkers have theorized communism as the movement of and for a human community, as a particular mode of being-in-the-world, as well as Camatte has done. Second, and related to the first point, Camatte understood profoundly that communism is not a form of government. Indeed, one could show that Marx also understood communism as an interminable process, and not as a government or as end state, in light of his definition in *The German Ideology*, for example, that communism is "not a stable state which is to be established, an *ideal* to which reality will have to adjust itself. We call communism the *real* movement which abolishes the present state of things."[168] In this way, we could argue that Camatte simply reads Marx correctly. In any case, Camatte's conception coincides well with the conception I have insisted upon in the present manifesto. In a beautiful essay from 1974, "Community and Communism in Russia," Camatte juxtaposes the claims of communism in Russia to the absence of community there, as a way to expose the fundamental contradiction:

> The Russian revolution and its involution are indeed some of the greatest events of our century. Thanks to them, a horde of thinkers, writers, and politicians are not unemployed. Among them is the first gang of speculators which asserts that the USSR is communist, the social relations there having been transformed. However, over there men live like us, alienation persists.[169]

---

167 We have been considering the privatization of social life variously throughout this book, but especially recall our analysis in Part II in relation to Habermas' theories of privatism from his *Legitimation Crisis* (Beacon Press, 1975).

168 Marx, *The German Ideology*, in *The Portable Karl Marx* (Penguin Books, 1983), p. 179.

169 Camatte, "Community and Communism in Russia" in *The Selected Works of Jacques Camatte* (Prism Key Press, 2011), p. 179.

This point calibrates the discussion well. We must speak of association beyond institutional forms, of association as a positive principle for the multifarious agendas of precarious communists. Why? Because, despite other differences, we understand that alienation and privatization are inextricably linked to the capitalist lifeworld, we understand that the social body has been deformed by the pathologies of withdrawal and disassociation. Following Camatte, no alienated lifeworld can be called "communist" because alienation is antithetical to community. Whereas, association in the form of voluntary, agonistic, therapeutic, and even joyful comings together can substantiate real moments of the *Gemeinwesen*, real communist moments. The real historical problem for communism has been its fleeting existence in saturnalias of *Gemeinwesen,* which form and dissipate too quickly.

And yet, the ideologically embroidered narrative about the grand old "communist" standoff against capitalism, survives in a more insidious form now than during the Cold War, because it has become part of a public consciousness that capitalists can safely take for granted, a public consciousness that assumes that the way forward will always take place within the limits of capital.

However, if the communist idea is recognized in those temporary human associations that have the affective effect of affirming or restoring our sense of dignity, then we can come into touch with communism as a possibility, as a desire. The psychic breakthrough we need might take the form of a question, or an epiphany: Is there any person who does *not* want, who does *not* cherish, communist human relations? If so, what would that mean, who would that be?

What does it mean to be a communist today? If this is imagined as some villainous thing, that a communist seeks to destroy your life as you know it, whether you like it or not, then what it means to be a communist would be defined as the exact contrary of the communist's real character. Now, we should confess the communist's destructive desires, even her or his desire to be brutally destructive when it comes to a life of increasingly fragile *dignity*, fleeting *autonomy*, and no enduring human *associations*. A communist is indeed unkind to such a state of affairs, wants to destroy alienation, and may well be an enemy of life as we know it, inasmuch as this is our life. But the most important qualification is our precariousness, for we are far too uncertain to try our hand at rearranging *your* life. So what does a communist do? We are active critical agents who can only entreat you – in as many creative ways as possible – to consider the conditions of life governed by capital. Yes, the conditions of such a life will also entreat you to condemn them, but a communist helps with the process.

2.
(Neo) Liberalism

It has become a commonplace amongst Leftists and radicals to criticize neoliberalism. Neoliberalism is a real movement, distinct from classical liberalism, and must indeed be criticized as a particular historical phenomenon. However, the fixation of the social sciences on the neoliberal restructuring of capital in the decades after World War II, particularly from the 1970s to the present, obscures the fact that classical liberalism is also a problem. We may well prefer liberalism to neoliberalism, and there are good reasons for such a preference, but a critique that singles out neoliberalism exculpates liberalism with too many pardoning distinctions.

Classical liberals from John Locke to John Rawls were *not* neoliberals. These philosophers bookend a long history of liberalism that called for clear limits to accumulation in the name of some conception of the common good or public justice.[170] In short, for classical liberals, the freedom of capital was neither the only nor the most important freedom. Nonetheless, liberals like Locke and Rawls accepted the possibility of achieving the common good or justice as fairness within the limits of capital and thus considered that the pursuit of justice was fully compatible with the pursuit of private property and wealth. The fact that "fair capitalism" is a contradiction in terms is never properly registered in the work of Rawls.

We could say that liberalism has neither understood the logic of capital, nor the history of capitalism. Marx sought to demonstrate this himself in his thoroughgoing critique of David Ricardo and Jean-Baptiste Say. In the 20th century especially, liberals rarely sought to study capitalism with any sustained critical attention, and typically began from a premise that accepted it. Already for Locke, the individual's conversion of common property into private property was a necessary precondition for the continuation of human life.

---

170 See Locke's Chapter 5 "Of Property" in *Two Treatises of Government* (Cambridge University Press and Mentor Books, 1965) and Rawls' Part II in *Justice As Fairness: A Restatement* (Harvard University and Belknap Press, 2001).

> Was it a Robbery thus to assume to himself what be-
> longed to all in Common? If such a consent as that was
> necessary, Man had starved, notwithstanding the Plenty
> God had given him. We see in *Commons*, which remain
> so by Compact, that 'tis the taking any part of what is
> common, and removing it out of the state Nature leaves
> it in, which *begins the Property*; without which the Com-
> mon is of no use.[171]

There are, of course, other problems, but liberalism's historic and ongoing assumption that first, life itself depends upon private property, and that second, fairness, equality, freedom, and other abstract virtues, are all perfectly compatible with or advanced by capitalism, is enough to make the exoneration of liberalism inexcusable.

Neoliberals rarely call themselves "neoliberals." The more common self-identifications are "liberal," "conservative," or even (especially in the US) "libertarian." All of these are typically "neoliberal." One of the most fascinating things about neoliberalism is that it is wholly accepted by representatives of supposedly opposing political parties. To be precise, then, I shall speak in this section of liberalism, by which I mean to include classical liberals from Locke to Rawls as well as "neo" variations on the theme.

Liberalism seeks to redress social and political grievances in ways that demonstrate the merits and secure the continued existence of the current social and political system. Classical liberals pursue more change, more reform, than classical conservatives do (we have to exclude neoconservatives here), but nothing revolutionary, illegal, riotous, or too contentious is ever *really* necessary from the liberal point of view. Liberalism already holds sway within the institutional and imaginal spaces of present-day capitalist societies. From the perspective of liberals and neoliberals, every reasonable demand is already a possible inroad, and "extremists" should be (or will eventually be) brought to recognize this practical fact.

Liberals and neoliberalism dominate the fields of economists, philanthropists, humanitarians, unions, ecumenical evangelical Christians, women's rights groups, LGBTQ activists, and reformers of every kind. Liberals are everywhere, and are increasingly conservative. As

---

171 Locke, John, *Two Treatises of Government* (Cambridge University Press and Mentor Books, 1965), Chapter 5, "Of Property," Section 28, p. 330.

a general rule, neoconservatives defend and follow the expansionist growth-logic espoused by neoliberalism, which is one of the best ways to distinguish neoconservatism from the classical conservatisms of Edmund Burke and Michael Oakeshott (i.e., Burke and Oakeshott's conservatism was not neoliberal).[172] Today, the free market fundamentalism of most conservatives is guided by neoliberalism.

Liberals want to keep everything that they are accustomed to within present-day society, and call for the improvement of the world only inasmuch as such improvement affirms the basic structure of the existing state of affairs. This is the conservative impulse of liberalism. As so-called "progressives," liberals call for change, but always and only change through existing legal channels, that is to say, change without structural transformation. To be fair, there is much sincerity in the liberal tradition, and liberals cannot one and all be accused of stupidity, malice, or deception (unlike so many of their right-wing counterparts); liberals really want the reforms they call for, sometimes they win them, and those reforms do make a difference in the lives of certain subsets of the affected populations.

Aside from its historical misunderstanding of capitalism, a history of apologetics, the greatest problem with liberalism is its unacknowledged utopianism and impracticality. The liberal ideology proliferates an understanding in which liberalism appears as the practical alternative to radicalism. If liberals can be accused of anything else, therefore, it would have to be of ideology.

It is counterintuitive to point out the utopianism and impracticality of liberalism, for these are the very charges that liberals usually level against their radical critics. Liberals have long viewed anarchists and communists as impractical utopians. But what are the realistic, practical goals of liberalism? On one major field of action, liberals seek to address problems by way of electing "better" men to solve them. If the present man is a good man, but ineffectual, then maybe he lacks resolve, fortitude, is being stymied by an oppositional congress, or is just bound up in a re-election campaign. The liberal thus holds out hope that his representative's last term will be the one where he will make the difference. Politics is not only about elections and institutional representation for liberals, but that is their

---

172 See Burke, Edmund, *Reflections on the Revolution in France* (Oxford University Press, 1993) and Oakeshott, Michael, "On Being Conservative" in *Rationalism in Politics and Other Essays* (Basic Books, 1962).

primary battlefield. If only we could get everything in place within the structures of governance, liberals believe, we could regulate, legislate, and acculturate our way *out of* racism, sexism, heterosexism, and classism, and *into* a world of social and economic justice. The cultural politics of liberalism is about increasing the resonance of liberal ideas, yet mostly in relation to recalibrating the electorate for the acceptance or rejection of executive and legislative action. In this way, the cultural politics of liberalism is always already a part of the campaigns of professional politicians, even when it appears to be non-institutional and autonomous. Is it really unfair to wonder if all these liberals who pine away for the liberatory achievements of professional politics have been paying any attention at all? They don't seem to notice the utopianism of their faith or the abysmal limitations of their political praxis, even in relation to the relative smallness of liberal aspirations, none of which are truly achieved by their methods. In light of these rather noncontroversial observations we can say that liberalism is impractical and utopian. Utopianism is not so bad, and could indeed be defended, when it is conscious of itself as utopian, but that is not the case with the liberal delusion.

There is enough variation among liberals to where one can find many who confess the frustrating limitations of their own theory and practice. Unfortunately, acknowledgement of these limitations is hardly dissuasive, and tends to lead down new avenues of unconscious utopianism. For example, many liberals readily acknowledge the long history of growing income inequality in capitalist societies, and many liberals understand that electoral methods of procedural democracy have been hijacked by moneyed interests. Yet, the liberal recommendation is to create a capitalist democracy uncorrupted by money. But isn't a capitalist democracy uncorrupted by money a contradiction in terms, and hasn't capitalist democracy been showing us this concretely since at least the Industrial Revolution?[173] Of course, liberals will cite efforts at campaign-finance reform, movements for public funding, and all kinds of convenient microscopic precedents, mostly failures, that pale by comparison to macropolitical trends, most recently demarcated by the signposts of accelerated privatization, super PACs and Citizens United vs. Federal Election Commission. Such persistence

---

173 An important contribution to answering this question was published in Charles A. Beard's classic study, *An Economic Interpretation of the Constitution of the United States* (The Free Press, 1986).

reveals the liberal ideology. If it weren't for ideology, liberals would have to confront the utopian impracticality of their position.

As mentioned in passing, utopianism is not to be condemned. Properly situated, utopianism can be a theoretical North Star. Utopian thought can liberate the social and political imagination, helping us to imagine the best of all possible worlds, without the delusion that we could make such worlds a reality, but rather, to measure our actual directions. When precarious communists are utopian, we are regulated by a countervailing realism; the utopianism of precarious communists is haunted by the facts of our own precarity. To the liberals we say: Be realistic, be communist!

Utopia useful for measurement to our world, but precarious communists don't fight for a utopia!

3.

Anarchism

We cannot reduce a long history of oppositions between anarchists and communists to nothing. This is a history with consequence. The disagreements between Marx and Proudhon and between Marx and Bakunin, raised critical issues in the debates of the 19th century that would take all of the next century to settle, and they have not yet been finally settled. But there is another long history, less sordid and less scandalous, which has been eclipsed by strong personalities and ideological bluster. Something must be said about it here.

Marx made some dangerous errors, among the worst of them his "Demands of the Communist Party in Germany," in addition to the others discussed in this book. But Marx also gave us the most systematic, rigorous, and exhaustive analysis of the history and tendencies of capitalism that he was capable of producing in a single lifetime, all of his intellectual energies ultimately given over to that task. Beginning at the age of 26, with the *Economic and Philosophic Manuscripts of 1844*, with an exploration of the basic building blocks of capitalism, until the posthumously published volumes of *Capital*, Marx invested a lifetime of attention to understanding capitalism with an overarching interest in its destruction, in the total reversal and replacement of its operational logic. When one reads the anarchist literature contemporaneous with Marx and with the early Marxism of the early 20th century, certain things are undeniable, assuming we are honest. Proudhon, Bakunin, Kropotkin, Malatesta, Goldman, and so many

[handwritten: Anarchists agree with 3 communist principles]

others, made dependable use of Marx's analyses of capitalism, so much
so that one could find them fully agreeable on three major grounds: (i)
the impossibility of an acceptable capitalist lifeworld; (ii) the possibility and desirability of a new world organized on *other* principles; (iii)
the necessity of revolution (although, many different and incompatible conceptions of revolution are at play in this history).

When, for example, one reads Errico Malatesta's small treasure of
a book, *At the Café: Conversations on Anarchism*, the analysis of capitalism and class follows Marx right up to the question of revolution,
at which point Malatesta distinguishes anarchism from communism
through a discussion of "free communism."[174] The first Russian edition of the Communist Manifesto was translated and widely circu-
lated by Bakunin in the 1860s, and Bakunin openly credited Marx's
intelligence and skill as a propagandist, even agreeing with Marx's
critique of Proudhon. Bakunin, of course, also had a complex relationship with Marx and Marxism. Bakunin joined the Geneva section of the First International, helped to create new branches in Italy
and Spain, and translated many of Marx's other works into Russian,
but was ultimately expelled from the International over disagreements
with Marx. Yet, only one year after his expulsion, Bakunin would admit: "Rarely can a man be found who knows so much and reads so
much, and reads so intelligently, as Marx... It goes without saying
that Marx read all the French socialists, from Saint-Simon to Proudhon, and it is well known that he hates the latter. Undoubtedly there
is a good deal of truth in the merciless critique he directed against
Proudhon."[175] We must acknowledge the existence of a long line of
fallings out, too, especially between Marx and Bakunin, and between
Marx and Proudhon, i.e., following Proudhon's explicit rejection of
Marx's insistence on "revolutionary action" in his letter to Marx of
May 17, 1846. At the same time, Proudhon advocated a very different
conception of revolution, in terms of a social transformation, which
he thought would be more enduring, albeit much slower: "I would
therefore prefer to burn property slowly with a small fire than to give
it new strength by carrying out a Saint Bartholomew's Night of the
Proprietors..."[176] In those days, anarchists were capable of critiquing

---

174 Malatesta, Errico, *At the Café: Conversations on Anarchism* (Freedom Press,
    2005), p. 65.

175 Bakunin, *Statism and Anarchy* (Cambridge University Press, 1990), p. 142.

176 See Proudhon, Pierre-Joseph, "Letter to Karl Marx" in *Property Is Theft! A*

Marx, while also crediting him for building the foundation on which anarchism could find a firmer footing.[177]

While disputes between communists and anarchists are undeniable and important, communists and anarchists have always had much agreement, much crosspollination in analysis and praxis, as well as theoretically formative relationships grounded in a broad normative consensus on the basic questions of capital. Today, the impetuses for the dissolution of old dichotomies are stronger than ever. There is an antidote to the categorical allergy of anarchists to communists and of communists to anarchists, and it is called philosophy, or if you prefer, the antidote is thinking-beyond-the-limits-of-ideology.

Despite this, the stubborn old allergies persist. The good news is that they cannot be taken very seriously. Let us consider a prominent example. Michael Hardt and Antonio Negri, who have made important contributions to the articulation and revitalization of Marxism, have retained a strange insistence on distinguishing an ideological divide that dissolves in their own work. They declare that it is their time, as communists, to give voice to the cry *"Big government is over!"* They acknowledge the old socialistic aspiration to use government to redistribute wealth, and they confess: *"Today, however, those times are over."* A few passages later, Hardt and Negri define the quest of the multitude, the new revolutionary subject position, as being a quest for *"autonomous self-government."*[178] No anarchist would disagree with this declaration from the two communists. Indeed, anarchism finds much resonance in many dimensions of Hardt and Negri's work, and many anarchists have made use of it. Hardt and Negri know this well enough to immediately anticipate the accusation that they are anarchists. They imagine the accusation and make the following preemptive rebuttal:

[handwritten: Too much ideology in Anarchist + Communist — they don't realise similarities]

> *That is not true. We would be anarchists if we were not* to speak (*as did Thrasymachus and Callicles, Plato's im-* *mortal interlocutors) from the standpoint of a materiality* *constituted in the networks of productive cooperation, in*

Pierre-Joseph Proudhon Anthology (AK Press, 2011), p. 164.

177 See also "Bakunin's Reminiscence" of Marx in *The Portable Karl Marx* (Penguin Books, 1983), p. 26 and Emma Goldman's *My Disillusionment in Russia* (Dover, 2003).

178 Hardt and Negri, *Empire* (Harvard University Press, 2001), p. 349.

other words, from the perspective of a humanity that is con-
structed productively, that is constituted through the "com-
mon name" of freedom. No, we are not anarchists but com-
munists who have seen how much repression and destruction
of humanity have been wrought by liberal and socialist big
governments.[179]

What is "the standpoint of a materiality constituted in the networks of productive cooperation?" What is *the perspective of a humanity that is constructed productively?* Do Hardt and Negri mean that they are not anarchists because they accept the materialist premises of Marx's political-economy? Have they not read the rich history of anarchism in which those very premises are also accepted, a history in which such premises are often accepted with a self-conscious debt to Marx? The perspective of a humanity constructed productively can be found throughout the history of anarchism, in the diverse writings of Lucy Parsons, Errico Malatesta, Peter Kropotkin, Charlotte Wilson, and Rudolph Rocker, just to name some obvious examples.

To be fair, many anarchists have made mistakes just as bad as (and worse than) Hardt and Negri's when it comes to ideologizing the divide between forms of communism. I say "and worse than" because many anarchists have become so sectarian amongst themselves, especially in the latter half of the 20th century, that they have produced a subaltern cottage industry of anarchist broadsides against anarchists. Anarchists have happily gotten lost in rather visceral attacks against those who share the rare distinction (rare when we consider the public sphere more widely) of radical aspirations against both the state and capital.[180]

The position that must be made clear here is that there is nothing to take seriously in Hardt and Negri's peculiar insistence that they *"are not anarchists but communists who have seen how much repression and destruction of humanity have been wrought by liberal and social-ist big governments."*[181] From Bakunin and Malatesta to the present,

---

179 Ibid., p. 350.
180 I am not going to catalogue this little cottage industry for readers, which would be no less a diversion here than it is in itself. But one can find it in many locations, i.e., in the published record of disputes between Murray Bookchin, John Zerzan, Bob Black, Hakim Bey, etcetera.
181 Hardt and Negri, op. cit., p. 350.

anarchists have always been communists who have seen how much repression and destruction of humanity have been wrought by governments. Indeed, the anarchist prescience about such repression and destruction by liberal and "socialist" governments defined them in the 19th century, when their theory of power only looked like a fearful wager. That very same theory vindicated the anarchists in the 20th century when it looked like a prophecy.

Today, we must understand that a communist who distrusts and rejects state power as destructive and repressive is very much an anarchist, just as every good anarchist is also much of a Marxist. No serious Marxist philosopher has ever accepted and defended every tenet of Marx's works, and many have even rejected major features of Marx's arguments, a tradition that goes back at least to Gramsci's essay "The Revolution Against *Capital*" and Lukács' denouement of orthodox, vulgar Marxists.[182]

If you want the anarchists to renounce Marxism and if you want the communists to renounce anarchism, get over it! We are too precarious for all of that.

In the name of autonomy, you can call yourself whatever you like, and by all means, explain yourself. Mis/recognition is often a serious political problem, and words do matter, but who has the power to permanently fix an identity to an ideologized concept and its name? Parents and states and Nazis and racists of every kind have tried, but their successes have inevitable, often catastrophic, expiration dates. We are slippery. We should not be in a rush to settle planes of becoming, planes of indeterminacy.

In *Anti-Oedipus: Capitalism and Schizophrenia*, Deleuze and Guattari famously discuss the body without organs (BwO), an idea borrowed from Antonin Artaud, expounded to mean a plane of indeterminacy, open possibilities, and the terrain of our becoming, of our fighting, of our losing and winning, a terrain on which we see ourselves as a body without organs. "Every coupling of machines, every production of a machine, every sound of a machine running, becomes unbearable to the body without organs. Beneath its organs it senses that there are larvae and loathsome worms, and a God at work

---

182 See Gramsci, Antonio, "The Revolution Against *Capital*" in *The Antonio Gramsci Reader: Selected Writings 1916 – 1935* (New York University Press, 2000), and Lukács, Georg, *History and Class Consciousness: Studies in Marxist Dialectics* (The MIT Press, 1999).

messing it all up or strangling it by organizing it."[183] Organs define the purposes of a body as a specific kind of machine, its constitutive parts make up a reference manual for what the machine is for, what it is designed to do. For the human machine, for the question of what the body can do and the question of what the body is made for, this comes down to a question of purpose. The BwO points to a subversive repurposing of the human person, of a human life. There are literal-physical possibilities, as in the cases of anorexia and transgender modifications, and there are figurative-existential possibilities, as in being for play instead of for work, or as in the feminist repurposing of what a woman can do. We can rethink our purposes, as the body without organs, and not leave the question up to God, up to production, or up to everyday life in capitalist societies. Guattari wrote about "becoming-woman" with an understanding of the subversive repurposing of gender.[184] A body without organs is the subject that is subject to change. In the political context of precarious communism, we need a communism as the body without organs of the "communists," that is, we need a new communist becoming, a becoming-ungovernable.

Precarious communists don't want to run the government. We have been running from or against governments everywhere in various ways for a very long time. And we cannot follow the lead of those fake libertarians who oppose the government, yet do not oppose capital, for they haven't noticed the colonization of government by capital, which is largely what has made government so dangerous. This is an old observation well documented by Cornelius Castoriadis and C. Wright Mills in the 1940s and 1950s, respectively, and by so many others since, but is so conveniently ignored by the fake libertarians of the world. All the more clear is our affection for the real libertarians, the anarchists.

If not the government, what do precarious communists want? We have already stated what precarious communists want. We want an actually existing everyday life full of dignity, autonomy, and human association, and *none* of the fleeting surrogates for these offered by capital.[185]

---

183 Deleuze and Guattari, *Anti-Oedipus: Capitalism and Schizophrenia* (Penguin Books, 2009), p. 9.

184 See Guattari, "Becoming-Woman" in *Hatred of Capitalism: A Semiotext(e) Reader* (Semiotext(e), 2001).

185 I have defined and discussed the meanings of dignity, autonomy, and association in Part III. Excurses, Section 1. Principles: *A., B., C.,* respectively.

IV.

Global Positioning of Precarious Communists

In Part II, we clarified the relationship between precarious communists and "communism."

Precarious communists will always fight for the gratification of immediate needs and aims, because living as well as possible matters, and because we cannot pretend that there are no worthy goals short of our greatest aspirations. If there is anything left of bourgeois morality, it is the delusion that we could and should live in line with "uncontaminated" principles. Precarious communists can fight against austerity and cast a cheap vote for a "lesser evil" without deciding anything against their good character. It is the liberal, not the precarious communist, who makes too much of reform. When we precarious communists support the unions we do so in the same spirit as we would accept a pay raise from a corporate employer, knowing full well that they will betray our interests at their convenience. Precarious communists are too precarious to be categorical on such subjects as these; we know that no substantive advance can be trusted or counted on, and we view every achievement as one nodal point in the development of an uncertain movement against capital, toward something more dignified, autonomous, and communist.

Precarious communism necessarily functions globally. Unlike "communism," precarious communism runs *no* risk of being calcified at the level of the nation-state. The growth-logic and tendencies of capital have always sought to exceed every border and every limitation, and capital has been effectively doing so since at least the mid-to-late 18th century. Capitalism carries with it the special form of precarity that we theorize as communist(s).

In Africa, capitalism has a variegated imperialist history, different in each country. But throughout the continent, a history of instability and neocolonialism have helped to construct the villain of a monolithic "West," which carries with it all the associations of highly technological capitalism. In the rural parts of some countries, such as in Ghana, westerners not only encounter a warm welcome, but even a discomfiting adulation. But capitalism has a changing and complex existence everywhere today, and in Africa, the more that capital appears as an *imposition* from the West, the more tenuous and volatile is its future. While this has historically been exemplified by social and political movements in sub-Saharan countries, like Angola, Congo, South Africa, and Mozambique, just to name a few, recent years have revealed defiant uprisings of precarious people in the Northern parts of the region.

Europe remains a place for radical currents and circuitry in both thought and praxis, and has always been a place (despite its changing boundaries) where one could reasonably expect an intellectual tradition that reckons and wrestles with Marx and Marxism. Europe does not, in other words, wholly blot out its own philosophical history, which is why one can find some of the most exemplary vindications of (and challenges to) Immanuel Kant's cosmopolitanism in the project of the EU and of "Europeanization." One of the most important things precarious communists may hope to see in Europe is the total implosion of its efforts to make capitalism more "socialistic," efforts which are today exacerbated by problems in the Eurozone and experimentations with austerity that reveal the precarity, and ultimately, the contradiction, of the state's commitment to public welfare in the context of capitalist crisis. The history of anarchism in Spain, autonomist currents from Italy, and the collective memories of *Solidarity* in Poland and the 1956 uprising in Hungary, are all fragments of a cultural and political history that lives on in multifarious ways. The celebrated insurrectionary history of France, including, of course, the

Paris Commune and the months of May and June in 1968, is an embodied characteristic of the most influential strains of radical French
theory, which functions as a kind of contagion that has infected philosophy around the world.

In Asia there is still much guarded enthusiasm about the promise
of capitalism, which derives largely (though not exclusively) from In-
dian and Chinese optimism, and which is not, of course, unanimous
within those regions. In fact, much of the optimism of capital is based
on images of these regions' soaring economic potentialities from outside. But Asia is also a place where the world finds concrete examples
that capitalism does not come along with democracy, that sometimes
the freedom of capital is expanded while democracy is undermined.[186]
Moreover, the entrenchment of China in the global network of production and debt reveals perhaps more than any other case that capitalism fosters less global interdependency than dependency, and less
global cooperation than competition.

In North and South America, we are interested in the development of new resistances to the US, which typically take the form of a
more hospitable resonance of communist ideas in countries like Bolivia, Mexico, Venezuela, and Brazil. Precarious communists are not
stupid about these so-called new "communist" governments or about
Bolivarian Revolution, and we can also see that communists have been
exposing the lies of the so-called "communism" there. More hopeful is the possibility for the re-emergence of a Zapatismo by other
names, and in new forms, which showed up in distinctive ways in the
indigenous movements of Bolivia, in the water war activism of Cocha-
bamba, and in Idle No More in Canada, for example.

In Antarctica, Australia, and New Zealand, we know there are indigenous movements too. Our ears and eyes are open to developments
from below, in both the Marxist sense, and in the geographic one.
But precarious communists are not naive enough to romanticize any
"revolutionary subject position," old or new – we do not romanticize
the indigenous, or the multitude, or even the precariat.

The logic of capital has run into many walls, but has always built
pathways of escape and expedience around or through those walls.
In many ways, capital has been running out – running out of ideas,

---

186 For an excellent book on this subject, see Tsai, Kellee S., *Capitalism Without
Democracy: The Private Sector in Contemporary China* (Cornell University Press,
2007).

geographic space, and time. Yet, the worst and easiest error of any new Marxian yarn is to spin another story about the inevitable limits of capital. Capital's own precarity does not guarantee anything in particular that is better.

The precarious of no country is the vanguard. There are no vanguards, and it is questionable if there ever were. A good student of Marx today must recognize one of the least convincing lines in his manifesto: "The Communists turn their attention chiefly to Germany, because that country is on the eve of a bourgeois revolution that is bound to be carried out under more advanced conditions of European civilization and with a much more developed proletariat than what existed in England in the 17th and France in the 18th century, and because the bourgeois revolution in Germany will be but the prelude to an immediately following proletarian revolution."[187] That Marx's prediction about proletarian revolution was wrong here is not the point. The point is about predictions in general, which can only be made precariously, and only ever could have been. Historical materialism accounts for almost any historical surprise, and thus never needed prediction as a vindication.

But precarious communists are inspired by every insurrectionary movement against the existing social and political order of things.

In the moment of these movements, precarious communists emphasize the central questions of capital, dignity, autonomy, association, and the prospects of each one at the time.

We always confront the pretensions of each political party. As Jacques Rancière so beautifully exposed, the democratic parties of all countries conceal their profound hatred for democracy.[188] We need not even reference the "communist" betrayals of communism from the 20th century in order to distrust representative democracy, for we know from the 18th century that representation was theorized and advanced as a safeguard *against* democracy.

Although precarious communists disdain to conceal their views and aims, the politics of subversion often call for clandestine, "offstage," or otherwise rhizomatic activities. But precarious communists never conceal the fact that their greatest aspirations cannot be attained within the limits of existing social conditions. We must be honest: The ruling classes tremble less at the threat of a communist revolution than

---

187 Marx, *The Communist Manifesto* (International Publishers, 1994), p. 44.
188 Rancière, *Hatred of Democracy* (Verso Books, 2006).

in the face of their own self-made insecurity. The precarious always have something to lose too, but for us, the loss has greater existential consequence (in both material and immaterial terms) – it is as serious as our lives. The undoing of our everyday anxieties is, in many ways, no less psychoanalytical than it is political. We have so many pathologies to confront, so many worlds to win.

To "unwind" does not always mean to breathe deeply, to meditate, to adapt, and to peaceably accept the world as it is. Sometimes, for example, a riot is a means of "psychic revolt" against the tightly-wound compression of everyday life, against racial profiling and police repression, against the generalized anxiety and repression of society and economy.[189] To "unwind" is even a common way to speak of the healthy response to work and its problems, where we imagine "unwinding" as a kind of precarious liberation from tension, a "decompression," a momentary freedom, a becoming-disentangled, at least until we're rewound once again. Yet, to unwind is also to cause an uncoiling, to literally undo what has been held in place under pressure by the demands of "making a living," by fears of dislocation, by the brutal logic of capital. At their best, the unwound are unruly, unpredictable, and ecstatic, giving off a pent up energy held in for too long. Worried of the world, unwind.

---

189 The concept of "psychic revolt" comes from Julia Kristeva. See Kristeva, *Revolt, She Said* (Semiotext(e), 2002), and Kristeva, *The Sense and Non-Sense of Revolt* (Columbia University Press, 2000).

Bibliography

Adorno, Theodor. 1983 [1966]. *Negative Dialectics*. E.B. Ashton, trans. New York: The Continuum Publishing Company.

Adorno, Theodor and Horkheimer, Max. 2011. *Towards a New Manifesto*. Rodney Livingstone, trans. London and New York: Verso.

Adorno, Theodor and Horkheimer, Max. 1997 [1944]. *Dialectic of Enlightenment*. John Cumming, trans. New York: The Continuum Publishing Company.

Arendt, Hannah. 1989 [1958]. *The Human Condition*. Chicago and London: The University of Chicago Press.

Autonomia: Post-Political Politics. 2007 [1980]. Lotringer and Marazzi, eds. Los Angeles: Semiotext(e).

Badiou, Alain. 2012. *Plato's Republic*. Susan Spitzer, trans. Cambridge, UK and Malden, MA: Polity Press.

Bakunin, Mikhail. 1990 [1873]. *Statism and Anarchy*. Marshall S. Shatz, trans. Cambridge, UK: Cambridge University Press.

Bakunin, Mikhail. 1983. "Bakunin's Reminiscence." In Kamenka, ed., *The Portable Karl Marx*. New York: Viking/Penguin Books.

Baudrillard, Jean. 1981. *For a Critique of the Political Economy of the Sign*. Charles Levin, trans. St. Louis: Telos Press.

Baudrillard, Jean. 1993 [1976]. *Symbolic Exchange and Death*. Iain Hamilton Grant, trans. London: Sage Publications.

Baudrillard, Jean. 2005 [1968]. *The System of Objects*. James Benedict, trans. London and New York: Verso.

Bauman, Zygmunt. 2007. *Liquid Times: Living in an Age of Uncertainty*. Cambridge, UK and Malden, MA: Polity Press.

Beard, Charles A. 1986 [1913]. *An Economic Interpretation of the Constitution of the United States*. New York: The Free Press.

Berardi, Franco "Bifo." 2009. *Precarious Rhapsody: Semiocapitalism and the Pathologies of the Post-alpha Generation*. Brooklyn: Minor Compositions/ Autonomedia.

Berardi, Franco "Bifo." 2009. *The Soul at Work: From Alienation to Autonomy*. Francesca Cadel and Giuseppina Mecchia, trans. Los Angeles: Semiotext(e).

Bernstein, Michèle. 2008. *All the King's Horses*. John Kelsey, trans. Los Angeles: Semiotext(e).

Bey, Hakim. 2003. *T.A.Z. The Temporary Autonomous Zone, Ontological Anarchy, Poetic Terrorism*. Brooklyn: Autonomedia.

Bookchin, Murray. 1986. *Post-Scarcity Anarchism: Second Edition*. Montreal and Buffalo: Black Rose Books.

Bookchin, Murray. 1997. *The Murray Bookchin Reader*. Janet Biehl, ed. London and Washington: Cassell.

Bookchin, Murray. 2007. *Social Ecology and Communalism*. Oakland, CA: AK Press.

Burke, Edmund. 1993 [1790]. *Reflections on the Revolution in France*. New York: Oxford University Press

Butler, Judith. 1990. *Gender Trouble: Feminism and the Subversion of Identity*. New York and London: Routledge.

Camatte, Jacques. 1995. *This World We Must Leave and Other Essays*. Brooklyn: Autonomedia.

Camatte, Jacques. 2011. *Capital and Community*. David Brown, trans. New York: Prism Key Press.

Camatte, Jacques. 2011. *The Selected Works of Jacques Camatte*. New York: Prism Key Press.

Castells, Manuel. 2000. *The Information Age: Economy, Society and Culture: Volume III: End of Millennium*. Oxford, UK and Malden, MA: Blackwell Publishers.

Castoriadis, Cornelius. *Political & Social Writings, Volume 1, 1946-1955: From the Critique of Bureaucracy to the Positive Content of Socialism*. 1988. David Ames Curtis, trans. Minneapolis: University of Minnesota Press.

Cornell, Drucilla. 1993. *Transformations: Recollective Imagination and Sexual Difference*. New York and London: Routledge.

Dauvé, Gilles and Martin, François. [1969, 1972, and 1974]. *The Eclipse and Re-Emergence of the Communist Movement: Revised Edition*. London: Antagonism Press.

Debord, Guy. 1995 [1967]. *The Society of the Spectacle*. Donald Nicholson-Smith, trans. New York: Zone Books.

Debord, Guy. 2001 [1985]. *Considerations on the Assassination of Gérard Lebovici*. Robert Greene, trans. Los Angeles: TamTam Books.

Debord, Guy and Wolman, Gil J. 2006 [1956]. "A User's Guide to Détournement." Ken Knabb, trans. In Knabb, ed. 2006.

Debord, Guy. 2006 [1957]. "Report on the Construction of Situations." Ken Knabb, trans. In Knabb, ed. 2006.

Debord, Guy. 2006 [1961]. "Perspectives for Conscious Changes in Everyday Life." Ken Knabb, trans. In Knabb, ed. 2006.

Debord, Guy. 2008 [1971]. "A Sick Planet." Donald Nicholson-Smith, trans. London: Seagull Books.

Deleuze, Gilles. 2012. *Gilles Deleuze From A to Z*. Noura Wedell and Hedi El Kholti, trans. Los Angeles: Semiotext(e).

Deleuze, Gilles and Guattari, Félix. 2009. *Anti-Oedipus: Capitalism and Schizophrenia*. Robert Hurley, Mark Seem, and Helen R. Lane, trans. New York: Penguin Books.

Dennett, Daniel C. 1991. *Consciousness Explained*. Boston: Back Bay Books.

Derrida, Jacques. 1982. *Positions*. Alan Bass, trans. Chicago: The University of Chicago Press.

Duncombe, Stephen and More, Thomas. 2012. *Open Utopia*. Wivenhoe, New York, and Port Watson: Minor Compositions/Autonomedia.

Dupont, Frére. 2007. *Species Being and Other Stories*. San Francisco: Ardent Press.

Dupont, Monsieur. 2009. *Nihilist Communism: A Critique of Optimism in the Far Left*. San Francisco: Ardent Press.

Falk, Richard. 1999. *Predatory Globalization: A Critique*. Malden, MA: Polity Press.

Fanon, Frantz. 1963. *The Wretched of the Earth*. Constance Farrington, trans. New York: Grove Press.

Federici, Silvia. 2012. *Revolution at Point Zero: Housework, Reproduction, and Feminist Struggle*. Oakland, CA: PM Press.

Foucault, Michel. 1980. *Power/Knowledge: Selected Interviews and Other Writings 1972-1977*. Colin Gordon, Leo Marshall, John Mepham, Kate Sopor, trans. New York: Pantheon Books.

Foucault, Michel. 1995. *Discipline and Punish: The Birth of the Prison*. Alan Sheridan, trans. New York: Vintage Books.

Foucault, Michel. 2008. *The Birth of Biopolitics: Lectures at the Collège de France, 1978-1979*. Graham Burchell, trans. London: Palgrave Macmillan.

Fraser, Nancy. 1997. *Justice Interruptus: Critical Reflections on the "Postsocialist" Condition.* New York and London: Routledge.

Friedman, Milton. 2002 [1962]. *Capitalism and Freedom.* Chicago and London: University of Chicago Press.

Gilman-Opalsky, Richard. 2008. *Unbounded Publics: Transgressive Public Spheres, Zapatismo, and Political Theory.* Lanham: Lexington Books.

Gilman-Opalsky, Richard. 2011. *Spectacular Capitalism: Guy Debord and the Practice of Radical Philosophy.* New York and London: Minor Compositions/Autonomedia.

Gilman-Opalsky, Richard. 2012. "Beyond the Old Virtue of Struggle: Autonomy, Talent, and Revolutionary Theory." (Rhizomes Journal, Number 24, 2012).

Gilman-Opalsky, Richard. 2013. "Unjamming the Insurrectionary Imagination: Rescuing Détournement from the Liberal Complacencies of Culture Jamming." (Theory in Action, Volume 6, Number 3, 2013).

Goldman, Emma. 2003 [1923]. *My Disillusionment in Russia.* New York: Dover Publications.

Graeber, David. 2009. *Direct Action: An Ethnography.* Oakland, CA: AK Press.

Gramsci, Antonio. 2000. *The Antonio Gramsci Reader: Selected Writings 1916 – 1935.* David Forgacs, ed. New York: New York University Press.

Grayling, A.C. 2011. *The Good Book: A Humanist Bible.* New York: Walker Publishing Company.

Guattari, Félix. 2001. "Becoming-Woman" in *Hatred of Capitalism: A Semiotext(e) Reader.* Kraus and Lotringer, eds. Rachel McComas and Stamos Metzidakis, trans. Los Angeles: Semiotext(e).

Habermas, Jürgen. 1975 [1973]. *Legitimation Crisis.* Thomas McCarthy, trans. Boston: Beacon Press.

Habermas, Jürgen. 1989 [1962]. *The Structural Transformation of the Public Sphere: An Inquiry into a Category of Bourgeois Society.* Thomas Burger, trans. Cambridge: The MIT Press.

Habermas, Jürgen. 2001 [1998]. *The Postnational Constellation: Political Essays.* Max Pensky, trans. Cambridge: The MIT Press.

Hardt, Michael and Negri, Antonio. 2001. *Empire.* Cambridge: Harvard University Press.

Hardt, Michael and Negri, Antonio. 2001. "What the Protesters in Genoa Want" in *On Fire: The Battle of Genoa and the Anti-Capitalist Movement.* London: One-Off Press.

Hardt, Michael and Negri, Antonio. 2004. *Multitude: War and Democracy in the Age of Empire.* New York: Penguin Books.

Harvey, David. 2007. *The Limits to Capital.* London and New York: Verso.

Hatred of Capitalism: A Semiotext(e) Reader. 2001. Kraus and Lotringer, eds. Los Angeles: Semiotext(e).

Hedges, Chris. 2009. *Empire of Illusion: The End of Literacy and the Triumph of the Spectacle.* New York: Nation Books.

Hegel, G.W.F. 1999. *Political Writings.* H.B. Nisbet, trans. Dickey and Nisbet, eds. Cambridge, UK: Cambridge University Press.

Hobbes, Thomas.1996 [1651]. *Leviathan.* Cambridge, UK: Cambridge University Press.

Hobsbawm, Eric. 2004. *The Age of Extremes: 1914-1991.* London: Abacus Publishing.

Holloway, John. 1998. "Dignity's Revolt." In Holloway and Peláez, eds., *Zapatistas! Reinventing Revolution in Mexico.* New York: Pluto Press.

Holloway, John. 2010. *Crack Capitalism.* London and New York: Pluto Press.

Holmes, Brian. 2008. *Unleashing the Collective Phantoms: Essays in Reverse Imagineering.* New York: Autonomedia.

Horkheimer, Max. 2002 [1941]. "The End of Reason," in Studies in Philosophy and Social Sciences, Vol. IX (1941) cited in Arato and Gebhardt, eds., *The Essential Frankfurt School Reader.* New York: The Continuum Publishing Company.

Horowitz, David and Laskin, Jacob. 2009. *One-Party Classroom: How Radical Professors at America's Top Colleges Indoctrinate Students and Undermine Our Democracy.* New York: Random House.

Jameson, Fredric. 2003. "Future City," in *New Left Review* # 21 (May-June 2003): 65-79.

Kant, Immanuel. 1998. *Groundwork of the Metaphysics of Morals.* Mary Gregor, trans. Cambridge, UK: Cambridge University Press.

Kant, Immanuel. 1999. *Political Writings.* H.B. Nisbet, trans. Dickey and Nisbet, eds. Cambridge, UK: Cambridge University Press.

Kincaid, Jamaica. 2000. *A Small Place.* New York: Farrar, Straus and Giroux.

Kristeva, Julia. 2000 [1996]. *The Sense and Non-Sense of Revolt.* Jeanine Herman, trans. New York: Columbia University Press.

Kristeva, Julia. 2002. *Revolt, She Said.* Brian O'Keeffe, trans. Los Angeles and New York: Semiotext(e).

Left Communism Reader: Sylvia Pankhurst, Herman Gorter, Anton Pannekoek and Jacques Camatte. 2013. New York: Prism Key Press.

Levin, Mark. 2009. *Liberty and Tyranny: A Conservative Manifesto.* New York: Simon & Schuster.

Locke, John. 1965 [1690]. *Two Treatises of Government*. New York, Toronto, and London: Cambridge University Press and Mentor Books.

Lukács, Georg. 1999 [1968]. *History and Class Consciousness: Studies in Marxist Dialectics*. Rodney Livingstone, trans. Cambridge: The MIT Press.

Malatesta, Errico. 2005. *At the Café: Conversations on Anarchism*. Paul Nursey-Bray, trans. London: Freedom Press.

Marx, Karl. 1978 [1845]. *Theses on Feuerbach*. In Tucker, ed. 1978.

Marx, Karl. 1983 [1845-46]. *The German Ideology*. Eugene Kamenka, trans. In Kamenka, ed. 1983.

Marx, Karl and Engels, Frederick. 1994 [1848]. *The Communist Manifesto*. Samuel Moore, trans. New York: International Publishers.

Marx, Karl and Engels, Frederick. 1967 [1848]. *The Communist Manifesto*. Samuel Moore, trans. New York: Penguin/Pelican Edition.

Marx, Karl. 1983 [1867]. *Capital: A Critique of Political Economy: Volume 1*. Eugene Kamenka, trans. In Kamenka, ed. 1983.

Marx, Karl. 2007 [1844]. *Economic and Philosophic Manuscripts of 1844*. Martin Milligan, trans., New York: Dover Publications

Marx, Karl. 2002 [1875]. *Critique of the Gotha Programme*. New York: International Publishers.

Mishel, Lawrence, Bernstein, Jared, and Allegretto, Sylvia: Economic Policy Institute. 2007. *The State of Working America 2006/2007*. New York: Cornell University Press.

Mishel, Lawrence, Bivens, Josh, Gould, Elise, and Shierholz, Heidi: Economic Policy Institute. 2012. *The State of Working America: 12th Edition. New York:* Cornell University Press.

Mill, John Stuart and Bentham, Jeremy. 1987. *Utilitarianism and Other Essays*. London and New York: Penguin Books.

Mills, C. Wright. 1956. *The Power Elite*. New York: Oxford University Press.

Negri, Antonio. 1991. *Marx Beyond Marx: Lessons on the Grundrisse*. Harry Cleaver, Michael Ryan, and Maurizio Viano, trans. New York: Autonomedia/Pluto Press.

Negri, Antonio. 2005 [1989]. *The Politics of Subversion: A Manifesto for the Twenty-First Century.* Cambridge, UK and Malden, MA: Polity Press.

Nussbaum, Martha and Sen, Amartya. 1993. *The Quality of Life*. New York: Oxford University Press.

Nussbaum, Martha. 2002 [1996]. "Patriotism and Cosmopolitanism." In Nussbaum and Cohen, eds., *For Love of Country?* Boston: Beacon Press, 2002.

Nussbaum, Martha. 2002. "Capabilities and Human Rights." In De Greiff and Cronin, eds., *Global Justice and Transnational Politics: Essays on the Moral and Political Challenges of Globalization*. Cambridge, MA: The MIT Press.

Oakeshott, Michael. 1962. *Rationalism in Politics and Other Essays*. New York: Basic Books.

O'Connor, James. 1998. *Natural Causes: Essays in Ecological Marxism*. New York: The Guilford Press.

Pannekoek, Anton. 2013 [1950]. *Workers' Councils*. New York: Prism Key Press.

Perlman, Fredy. 1992. *Anything Can Happen*. London: Phoenix Press.

Perlman, Fredy. 2007 [1961]. *The New Freedom: Corporate Capitalism*. New York: Southpaw Culture and Factory School.

Pignarre, Philippe and Stengers, Isabelle. 2011. *Capitalist Sorcery: Breaking the Spell*. Andrew Goffey, trans. New York: Palgrave Macmillan.

Plato. 1991 [*circa* 380 BC]. *The Republic of Plato: Second Edition*. Allan Bloom, trans. New York: Basic Books.

Proudhon, Pierre-Joseph. 1994 [1840]. *What is Property?* Donald R. Kelley and Bonnie G. Smith, trans. Cambridge, UK: Cambridge University Press.

Proudhon, Pierre-Joseph. 2011. *Property Is Theft! A Pierre-Joseph Proudhon Anthology*. Iain McKay, ed. Edinburgh, Oakland, and Baltimore: AK Press.

Rancière, Jacques. 2006. *Hatred of Democracy*. Steve Corcoran, trans. London and New York: Verso Books.

Rawls, John. 2001. *Justice As Fairness: A Restatement*. Cambridge: Harvard University and Belknap Press.

Sassen, Saskia. 1996. *Losing Control? Sovereignty in an Age of Globalization*. New York: Columbia University Press.

Sassen, Saskia. 1999. *Globalization and Its Discontents: Essays on the New Mobility of People and Money*. New York: The New Press.

Scott, James C. 1990. *Domination and the Arts of Resistance: Hidden Transcripts*. New Haven and London: Yale University Press.

Singer, Peter. 1993. *Practical Ethics: Second Edition*. Cambridge, UK: Cambridge University Press.

Sombart, Werner. 1976. *Why is there no Socialism in the United States?* Patricia M. Hocking and C.T. Husbands, trans. White Plains, NY: M.E. Sharpe.

Smith, Adam. 2009 [1776]. *The Wealth of Nations*. Blacksburg: Thrifty Books.

Thoreau, Henry David. 1993 [1849]. *Civil Disobedience and Other Essays.* New York: Dover Publications.

Touraine, Alain. 1971. *The Post-Industrial Society: Tomorrow's Social History: Classes, Conflicts and Culture in the Programmed Society.* New York: Random House.

Tsai, Kellee S. 2007. *Capitalism Without Democracy: The Private Sector in Contemporary China.* Ithaca and London: Cornell University Press.

UNDP: UN Human Development Report 1999: Tenth Anniversary Edition. New York and Oxford: Oxford University Press.

UNDP: UN Human Development Report 2005: International Cooperation at a Crossroads: Aid, Trade and Security in an Unequal World. New York and Oxford: Oxford University Press.

UNDP: UN Human Development Report 2006: Beyond Scarcity: Power, Poverty and the Global Water Crises. New York: Palgrave Macmillan.

UNDP: Africa Human Development Report 2012: Towards a Food Secure Future. New York: United Nations Publications.

Vaneigem, Raoul. 1983. *The Book of Pleasures. John Fullerton, trans.* London: Pending Press.

Vaneigem, Raoul. 1998. *The Movement of the Free Spirit.* Randall Cherry and Ian Patterson, trans. New York: Zone Books.

Vaneigem, Raoul. 2003 [1967]. *The Revolution of Everyday Life.* Donald Nicholson-Smith, trans. London: Rebel Press.

Vaneigem, Raoul. 2003. *A Declaration of the Rights of Human Beings: On the Sovereignty of Life as Surpassing the Rights of Man.* Liz Heron, trans. London: Pluto Press.

Virilio, Paul. 2006 [1977]. *Speed and Politics: An Essay on Dromology.* Marc Polizzotti, trans. Los Angeles: Semiotext(e).

Virilio, Paul. 2009 [1980]. *The Aesthetics of Disappearance.* Philip Beitchman, trans. Los Angeles: Semiotext(e).

Virilio, Paul. 2012. *The Administration of Fear.* Ames Hodges, trans. Los Angeles: Semiotext(e).

Virno, Paolo. 1996. "The Ambivalence of Disenchantment." In Virno and Hardt, eds., *Radical Thought in Italy: A Potential Politics.* Minneapolis and London: University of Minnesota Press.

Warner, Michael. 2000. *The Trouble with Normal: Sex, Politics, and the Ethics of Queer Life.* Cambridge: Harvard University Press.

Weinman, Michael. 2007. *Pleasure in Aristotle's Ethics.* New York: The Continuum Publishing Company.

Wilson, Charlotte M. 2000. *Anarchist Essays.* London: Freedom Press.

Zerzan, John. 2002. *Running on Emptiness: The Pathology of Civilization.* Los Angeles: Feral House.

Žižek, Slavoj. 2012. *Less Than Nothing: Hegel and the Shadow of Dialectical Materialism.* London and New York: Verso.

Minor Compositions

Forthcoming:

Lives of the Orange Men – Major Waldemar Fydrich
FutureChe – John Gruntfest & Richard Gilman-Opalsky
State in Time – Irwin
Islam & Anarchism – Mohamed Jean Veneuse
A Very Careful Strike – Precarias a la Deriva
Art, Production and Social Movement – Ed. Gavin Grindon
Hypothesis 891 – Colectivo Situaciones
Learn to Listen – Carlos Lenkersdorf
A Short Philosophical Dictionary of Anarchism from
    Proudhon to Deleuze – Daniel Colson

As well as a multitude to come...

CPSIA information can be obtained at www.ICGtesting.com
Printed in the USA
BVOW04s0233300614

683BV00002B/6/P